A Black Woman for President

A Black Woman for President

Shirley Chisholm, Carol Moseley Braun, and Kamala Harris

Dianna N. Watkins-Dickerson

University Press of Mississippi / Jackson

The University Press of Mississippi is the scholarly publishing agency of
the Mississippi Institutions of Higher Learning: Alcorn State University,
Delta State University, Jackson State University, Mississippi State University,
Mississippi University for Women, Mississippi Valley State University,
University of Mississippi, and University of Southern Mississippi.

www.upress.state.ms.us

The University Press of Mississippi is a member
of the Association of University Presses.

Wanda Coleman, "American Sonnet 61" from *Wicked Enchantment: Selected Poems*.
Copyright © 2020 by The Estate of Wanda Coleman.
Reprinted with the permission of The Permissions Company, LLC
on behalf of Black Sparrow / David R. Godine, Publisher, Inc., godine.com.

Any discriminatory or derogatory language or hate speech regarding race,
ethnicity, religion, sex, gender, class, national origin, age, or disability
that has been retained or appears in elided form is in no way an endorsement
of the use of such language outside a scholarly context.

Copyright © 2025 by University Press of Mississippi
All rights reserved
Manufactured in the United States of America

∞

Publisher: University Press of Mississippi, Jackson, USA
Authorised GPSR Safety Representative: Easy Access System Europe -
Mustamäe tee 50, 10621 Tallinn, Estonia, *gpsr.requests@easproject.com*

Library of Congress Cataloging-in-Publication Data

Names: Watkins-Dickerson, Dianna N. author
Title: A Black woman for president : Shirley Chisholm, Carol Moseley Braun,
and Kamala Harris / Dianna N. Watkins-Dickerson.
Description: Jackson : University Press of Mississippi, 2025. |
Includes bibliographical references and index.
Identifiers: LCCN 2025025411 (print) | LCCN 2025025412 (ebook) |
ISBN 9781496859389 hardback | ISBN 9781496859396 trade paperback |
ISBN 9781496859402 epub | ISBN 9781496859419 epub |
ISBN 9781496859426 pdf | ISBN 9781496859372 pdf
Subjects: LCSH: Chisholm, Shirley, 1924–2005 | Moseley-Braun, Carol, 1947– |
Harris, Kamala, 1964– | Rhetoric—Political aspects—United States |
Womanism—United States | Political oratory—Social aspects—United States |
Women presidential candidates—United States | African American women politicians |
Presidential candidates—United States |
BISAC: LANGUAGE ARTS & DISCIPLINES / Rhetoric |
POLITICAL SCIENCE / Women in Politics
Classification: LCC PN239.P64 W38 2025 (print) | LCC PN239.P64 (ebook)
LC record available at https://lccn.loc.gov/2025025411
LC ebook record available at https://lccn.loc.gov/2025025412

British Library Cataloging-in-Publication Data available

Contents

Acknowledgments vii

Introduction: Beyond the Pulpit and the Pew: Searching for Womanist Rhetors on Political Platforms 3

Chapter 1: Bringing a Purse to the Political Stage: Introducing Womanist Rhetorical Theory as a Metatheory for Communication Studies 17

Chapter 2: "Never Ask for Permission to Lead": Reimagining Presidential Speeches Through Womanist Rhetorical Theory 27

Chapter 3: "I Ran Because Somebody Had to Do It First": The Presidential Campaign Announcement Speech of Congresswoman Shirley Chisholm 60

Chapter 4: "Defining Myself . . . Is One of the Most Difficult Challenges I Face": The Presidential Campaign Announcement Speech of Senator Carol Mosley Braun 85

Chapter 5: "Dreamers Cannot Afford to Sit Around": The Presidential Campaign Announcement Speech of Senator Kamala Devi Harris 109

Chapter 6: "Daring to be Herself": Using Black Women's Presidential Campaign Speeches to Create a Theoretical Imperative to Shape the World and a Quasi-Optimistic Future 132

References 145

Index 153

Acknowledgments

> Do the work your soul must have.
> —KATIE GENEVA CANNON, AUTHOR OF *KATIE'S CANNON*

> If there's a book that you want to read but it hasn't been written yet, then you must write it.
> —TONI MORRISON, AUTHOR OF *A MERCY*

Black women's voices have long been ignored. Whether they find themselves preaching in pulpits, pushing political platforms, or within public podiums, their voices have been noted for their ability to entertain and perform as the center of spectacle but have not always been taken seriously. With every speech, sermon, song, and soliloquy, their aptitude and adroitness in crafting their own persuasive concepts in rhetoric, and other theoretical frameworks whether in public or in private, have not been celebrated *enuf*. My soul has worked tirelessly to craft a project written with them in mind, without borrowing from or simply improving a white model that in some way reifies interest in patriarchy and white supremacy. For me, it just doesn't work, nor does it have to. So, along with my grandfather's wisdom to "trust God and yourself" and the indomitable spirit of my grandmother, I am convinced it is my fierce faith, the prayers of the saints, and the giants upon whose shoulders I stand that this work has been put within my reach. I have written a book that I hope would make my ancestors proud, theorizing through the act of singing a Black girl's song . . . of possibilities. But I did not do it alone.

To my husband, Dr. Dennis C. Dickerson Jr., my son Dennis Clark Dickerson III (better known as "D3"), my mother Jerrie Y. Watkins, and my aunt M. Dianne Watkins, please know that I am forever grateful for your constant love, affection, understanding, and push to complete this work. My mentors Drs. Andre E. Johnson, Antonio de Velasco, Gray Matthews, and Shelby

Crosby have been not only excited about my work but consistent in their critiques and encouragement to better the eventual product. Last minute phone calls, motivational talks, and reading over drafts allowed me to lean on other scholars like Dr. Dennis C. Dickerson Sr. and sister-friends to get this work to completion. Cecelia Olusola Tribble, Serita Baysmore, Ketara Gray, Lauren Aqeel Juzang, and Drs. Christina Dickerson Cousin, Noor Gazal Aswad, and Katrina Brown, you were in my life for not simply a season but a reason. Your encouragement at very crucial points of this work is not in vain. Not everyone has this amount of support, and I am forever grateful. I am especially thankful for the women I write about, sight/cite, and remember in this text. Whether residing somewhere "on the other side of glory" or in the Blair House as the first Black woman vice-president of the United States of America, may your theoretical genius and political perseverance be known to the masses. Thank you for "daring to be yourself."

Last but certainly not least, I write for Dionne Yvonne. She is the womanish daughter that chose me to be her mother. I birthed her amid the editing process and COVID-19 pandemic. I hope we can all one day live in a world where everyone wants, desires, needs, and most importantly *believes* in the promise of "a Black woman for president." Maybe, that will be you, sweet girl.

Still, God is faithful.

A Black Woman for President

Introduction

Beyond the Pulpit and the Pew

Searching for Womanist Rhetors on Political Platforms

> I want history to remember me ... not as the first black woman to have made a bid for the presidency of the United States but as a black woman who lived in the 20th century and who dared to be herself. I want to be remembered as a catalyst for change in America.
> —SHIRLEY CHISHOLM

And it does. Communication theory centering the epistemological realities, phenomenological truths, and ontological station of Black womanhood should mark Shirley Chisholm not only as the unbought, unbossed, and *unbothered* political candidate that brought a folding chair to every table denying her presence but also as a womanist theoretical foremother (Watkins-Dickerson and Johnson 2019). In fact, standing upon the shoulders of Jarena Lee, Maria Stewart, Anna Julia Cooper, Charlotta Amanda Spears Bass, and countless others coming to voice as rhetors in public spaces, Chisholm not only became the first Black woman to make a convincing bid for the American presidency for a major American political party but pushed forth a womanist rhetorical style, opening the way for others. By remaining true to her audience and centering her focus within the ideological pillars of the Black community, her discourse not only was *womanish* in nature but spoke to and beyond her own rhetorical situation, as well as the rhetorical conditions imposed upon her. Explicitly and inexplicitly, her political tenure still captivates and necessitates study from audiences across the world by demonstrating just a foretaste of Black women's formidable modes of speaking truth to power amid contentious, and often noxious, exigencies. These "powers that be" far too often undermine Black women's ability to speak in the public square as normatively accepted citizens, at minimum, let alone credible political candidates for the American presidency, at best. In large part, Chisholm is not simply positioned as a womanist rhetor in this text because of her Blackness and womanhood but because of the conceptual precedents she embraced. She figuratively brought folding chairs for other Black women (and their allies) to sit at political tables, stand on platforms, and even create their own spaces to work toward thriving, even though she did not live to see each glass ceiling break ever so slightly. Certainly, her bid for the White House paved the way, most recently, for Vice-President Kamala Harris and continues to largely shape the ways in which Black women press their way toward the political sphere.

Womanist rhetorician Toniesha Taylor argues, "Womanist rhetoric is defined within the African American woman's experiences as a primary cultural discourse. As a primary cultural discourse womanist rhetoric contains three pillars: authentic womanist voice, gendered cultural knowledge and ethical discourse for salvation" (2009, 2). Building from Taylor, I contend that a womanist rhetor emphasizes that the privilege, power, prowess, and inherent pleasure (passively or actively derived from the pain of others) embedded within the core of whiteness is a fundamental problem; contends patriarchy is only wholly accessible to white men; and understands Black women's femininity is negotiated neither by the standards upheld by the cult of true womanhood/domesticity nor Republican motherhood but outside of it and survival is only available when she introduces options to include herself within her version of the *beloved* community. These options work toward holistic everyday thriving in the *here and now* and extend beyond generally perceived notions of rhetorical, theological, political, and institutional respectability or favor for things perceived to be "good" under the umbrella of the white gaze. This said, Black women's voices hold within them a universal imperative that determines that "all God's chillun got wings," "God is no respecter of persons," and, most importantly, "God don't like ugly." To be clear, whereas this spiritual aspect of womanist thought is not necessarily centralized within a Western Christian doctrine, it does consider cosmologically related ideologies held within the lenses of Afrocentricity, Black liberation theology, and even the righteous indignation of ordinary women. These are women we can find at family gatherings, religious meetings, and everyday jobs.

For instance, literary greats like Alice Walker used characters and story lines to shape, challenge, define, and imagine Black womanhood beyond the normative gaze. Figures in *The Color Purple* like Celie demonstrated the maligned and mistreated women who were forced by libeled outplays of Black patriarchy to concede and retreat, while the Mrs. Sophia's of the world shouted *"Hell no!"* What is read as an ostentatious outburst serves to refute the entitlement of white femininity while simultaneously fighting what, in the text, seemed to be all of Jim/Jane Crow through an army of one. Before Miss Millie's racist offense and beside Mrs. Sophia's incessant defense, womanist rhetorical theory's goal is to offer and dispense discursive recompense for scholars, students, activists, mothers, daughters, nieces, othermothers, and the myriad of Black women (and those that love them into their whole selves without violence) to come to voice. This is not to say that womanist theory, writ large, antagonizes or approaches feminist concepts with outright contempt and theoretic rejection but that it realizes and recognizes that far too often white women are automatically afforded safety even when they are the threat. Like Mrs. Sophia's story line demonstrates, in spite of the calculated, rationalized, measured experiences and decisions within and outside of white society, the white supremacist fashions of "saviorhood" and salvation are never calling cards handed out to them in tense or disparaging situations. Even when the best offers for bridging the racial gap are given to expand the scope of theoretical inquiry, the depths of expanding the notion of diversity, equity, and inclusion still can be usurped. As such, despite any communal sensibilities held and shared within and outside of the heteropatriarchal constructs of womanhood, motherhood, and femininity, whether normalized or expanded broadly, Black women simply are never allowed the space to live into this definition of being.

Womanist rhetorical theory, then, holds space for audible "nos" to address the *hell and high water* circling around the Black women who feel the intangible, see the invisible, and still can bear witness to the welts and lashes this evil *still* leaves, no matter how loud their cries of defense and terror and angst go ignored. It is a space where the demands of rhetorical criticism and phenomenography meet to combine forces in effort to ask and then offer answers to the question, "What is *really* going on?"

What is *really* going on in the midst of educational and police reform? What is *really* going on as Black neighborhoods are being gentrified? What is *really* going on as Black women are four times more likely to die in childbirth? What is *really* going on as Black women are one of the most educated racial groups in the country, but Briana Taylor's killers are only now answering for their crimes? What is *really* going on as the first Black woman serving as vice-president of the United States of America feels not only the weight and capacity of white supremacist instigation as she works to oversee lawmaking in Congress without receiving typical protections and procedures of political decorum traditionally demanded of her position? No matter the scenario, the womanist rhetor does not quit, nor does she allow frivolous attempts to determine and thereby dismiss what is being said or pushed as a primary issue, how it is constructed or deconstructed, and the violent implications and/or applications thereof. Womanist rhetors ask the difficult questions and are proud and unyielding in their quest for justice and thriving and peace and reform and *more*. Womanist rhetors go behind the curtain, so to speak, and delve into "deeper shades of purple."

Such a composite query to understand "what is *really* going on" is offered not by singer Marvin Gaye's 1971 R&B hit song but by the strident critical engagement championed by those like Ms. Shelly and other *seemingly* ordinary Black women, who normative structures would deem unnecessary to notice. These are women employed by institutional systems not created with them in mind yet deployed by communities fiercely maintaining and defending their humanity. Like many (potentially) missed and overlooked on the margins, Ms. Shelly was a childcare associate at Vanderbilt University who would give a last-minute hair fix before a date and in the next order deliver cleverly worded challenges to authority figures who may have been degreed and certified through educational and class status but knew little to nothing about the life beat of the organizations they lead on the supervisory flowchart. She, and others like her, would (and still do) dutifully care for the other Black women around her by calling "a thing a thing" before the witness of popular memes highlighting spiritual counselor and relationship mediator Iyanla

Vanzant—all while emotionally navigating her impending physical blindness. Ms. Shelly was the first to ask, "What is *really* going on?" during not-so-random inspections, criticisms of our ability to care for the children under our charge, and even the Republican challenge of former president Barack Obama's political legitimacy from surrounding caregivers (and news media pundits), all in the same conversation set. She had "sight beyond sight" and a way of knowing actively crippling the typically accepted and anticipated conclusions of Black women's capacity to think and adapt in the midst of misogynoir, no matter the encroachment on her personhood. Ms. Shelly's witness is only a mere example of countless *ordinary* Black women with similar vision and understanding without the typical degrees, certifications, or other normative ways society defines knowledge and insight.

Lessons from those like Ms. Shelley demonstrate the always and already circulating violation of humanity thrust upon the duality of everyday Blackness and femaleness. In many ways, this "epistemological privilege," or insightful, specially acquired knowledge through (sometimes violent and vile) lived experience enables them the only "proper" theoretical lens to pinpoint (and ultimately navigate) the various rhetorical emergencies and nefarious discursive denials constructed by white patriarchal violence. What is considered by some to be a lack of public distinctions and purposeful degrees neither diminishes nor dissuades their intellectual capacity. As such, theirs is a deeper understanding and more vociferous and more poignant critique of a world that does not love the fullness of Creation but *must* work far harder to be seen, to be heard, and to weave a web for others within her community to remember. Or, as womanist theologian Diana L. Hayes argues, "Somehow, [these women] wove a tapestry of strength and protection and constructed shoes made for walking in unknown worlds" (2010, 2). Consequently, the words (and worlds) of ordinary Black women from everyday life are what serve as the heartbeat and core of womanist intellectual thought. It is what frames the womanist rhetor, no matter the audiences she is working to remember, reconstruct, reimagine, and reclaim. Such utterances urgently, rightly, and righteously reframe and reimagine the dictates of conventionally canonized communicative culture, calling it a lie, not simply a half-truth, much like the "devil himself."

This book rhetorically purposely commands space for womanist theoretical framing in the field of communication by simultaneously navigating the use of scholarly semantics and contentedly foregrounding the importance of wading through cultural colloquialisms and linguistically relevant discursive space at the same time. By ushering in a decidedly womanist essence to underpin the scope of my academic inquiry, the self is validated as a widely informed rhetorical critic (Davis 1998) and capable cultural reader (Bobo 1995). Thus, I uphold the theory I am also utilizing, exploring, and outlining. In this manner, the Black women studied are upheld in ways where they are charting their own discursive destinies as political candidates, with special attention to the ways their speeches follow a particular brand of style. Yet what is paramount to perceive in each chapter are two primary goals of my analysis: (1) charting the implications and phenomenological particularities of womanist rhetorical theory as a reliable, legitimate field of inquiry within communication studies, and (2) applying the considerations of womanist rhetorical theory to Black women's political campaigns, with specific consideration of three announcement speeches for the office of president of the United States.

THREE BLACK WOMEN FOR PRESIDENT:
A NEW ERA IN THE AMERICAN PRESIDENCY

Shirley Anita St. Hill Chisholm. Carol Elizabeth Moseley Braun. Kamala Devi Harris. At the time of writing this text, only three women of African descent have given successfully recognized bids by a major political party for the office for president of the United States of America. So far, none of them have made it to the White House as commander in chief. Yet now, Vice-President Harris has shattered the mold of white, male leadership as the first woman and person of color (African and Asian descent) to be chosen for such a prestigious and powerful federal position along with the international authority and prestige it brings. While former Congresswomen Lenora Fulani, PhD, and Cynthia McKinney were candidates for the New Alliance Party in 1988 and the Green Party in 2008, respectively, the rhetorical trajectories of Chisholm, Moseley Braun, and Harris in their quest to achieve the nomination for the Democratic Party has gained them not only national coverage but international prominence and historical precedence. However, while the three women considered in this text produced political personas that are still of note today, they did not become candidates for the Democratic Party. Yet there was a Black woman selected to head an American political party, albeit a minority interest group before all of these.

Charlene Mitchell became the presidential candidate of the Communist Party USA in 1968. Stationed in Boston, her campaign stood within a party maligned by the McCarthy era and overshadowed by her race, her gender, and the party's radical political agenda. As a Black radicalist heavily influenced by anticolonialist and Cold War–era politics, undoubtedly, Mitchell, as a Black woman rhetor, played a pivotal role in charting a path for the women broadly considered. While it is not the express purpose of this text to consider the political communication and rhetorical trajectory of Mitchell, Fulani, or McKinney, I cannot overstate the inherent importance that exists in recognizing them as forerunners of the role of Black women who voiced their wish to run and did so in their respective political party. In fact, Fulani was the first Black woman to be listed on the ballot of each state in the country (Fulani 1992). Certainly, each woman drastically changed the course of American politics by creating rhetorical personas that resonated with their personal core values and their campaigns, which include a wide range of speeches, media appearances, advertising, slogans, sayings, and more immediately invoking the ideas and ideals of the Afrocentric idea of Sankofa.

Sankofa expresses a desire to look back to honor the past with efforts to understand the present while imploring for a parameter of hope for the future. It is the remembering and retelling of the story—not only as it happened but, more importantly, how it was experienced by the community holding its memory—that are central to this concept. The mere existence and efforts of those communal memories also call into being the ever-encompassing philosophy of *nommo* in spaces where Black rhetors exist and *thrive*. While *nommo* underscores the power of the spoken word, which necessitates the presence of spirit, community, balance, and even honor (Hamlet 1988, 91), its pervasiveness in moments of Sankofa builds a distinct discursive bridge between the past, present, and future in Black-centered rhetorical space. These considerations underscore the womanist tenets, tactics, and theoretical perspective used throughout this text. Furthermore, these (almost) kairos moments when Black women come to voice in the sphere of politics stand firmly outside of normative perspectives in many ways reject and re-create (without need or desire to reform) white, heteronormative viewpoints of how to study, write, and theorize ways toward thriving civically. At its heart, understanding and underscoring the importance of Sankofa and *nommo* in the realm of womanist communication studies helps us, as cultural readers, social participants, politically knowledgeable individuals, and everyday citizens, foreground what it means to study the discourse of Black women in general and specifically the speeches of Black women in politics.

This study concurrently explores political communication by embracing a womanist perspective. It uses this approach in order to build (with the hope of expanding) a rhetorical history of Black women rhetors; how these rhetors construct audiences who consider them to be commendable contenders for the American presidency; and, ultimately, how these theorizations should be captured, critiqued, and canonized outside of normative, white communication conceptualizations. Hence, *naming* all of these women and others in this text sights and cites their will and works, further legitimizing their hard-wrought role as civic leaders. Recognizing Black female political leaders through such an approach also stresses the agency necessary for them to believe in re-creating a path and new era of the American presidency. Such a tangible kindling of this rhetorical history can become a precedent for other women to follow in local, state, and federal campaigns in the future. Thus, planted at the precipice of two distinct avant-garde movements in Black Christianity and culture (Black liberation theology and the Black Arts Movement) cradled in her Bedford-Stuyvesant neighborhood in January 1972, then congresswoman Shirley Chisholm made history by being recognized as the first Black woman to make a viable run for presidential office in the pulpit of Concorde Baptist Church. Thirty-two years later, then US senator Carol Moseley Braun of Illinois was introduced by her son Matthew on the campus of Howard University to give a speech articulating her presidential aspirations. Following their lead is former California senator Kamala Harris, who finished her term serving as the vice-president of the United States of America in January 2025. First announcing her objective in front of *Good Morning America*'s live audience on Martin Luther King Day in 2019, Harris officially delivered a speech outlining her intent to run for office in front of the Oakland City Hall building.

Arguably, the specific location of these three Black women's announcement speeches presumes and assumes several things. These include, but are not limited to, the organization of their content; discursive patterns and vernacular, or the lack thereof; how they construct a particular audience; and, essentially, what that eventual audience believes most important to demonstrate who is the best political representation and presentation for the highest office in the country. For the women of this text, their locations held deep historical significance. Based on the specific context of such deeply meaningful and relevant locations serving as backdrop along with the communities behind them, Chisholm's, Moseley Braun's, and Harris's presidential campaign announcement speeches hold a deep well of information ripe for critique and consideration. They are far beyond what they seem to be on the surface. Furthermore, particularly thinking through the fact that these were Black women on the road to the White House, their rhetoric is not only built upon critically constrained, constricted, and (at times) convoluted texts at their disposal, but their lives, personas, and speech construction were contextualized by political ideals forged by personal and professional experiences. In many ways, it must also stand precariously against, before, and beyond the pretext of tripartite oppression permanently inscribed upon their bodies by society.

Womanist literary theorist Clenora Hudson-Weems (1989) argues, "The history of the Africana woman reveals her peculiar predicament within the dominant culture as a victim of a tripartite form of oppression, racism, classism, and sexism, respectively. Since American slavery, she and the Africana man have experienced much brutality; however, her womanhood has placed her in an even more vulnerable position" (192). Even as Black women "move up in the world" of business, politics, education, and other realms of status in Western society, their experiences are still marked by a historical precedence of sufferings underscored by the laws that built this country. Brandishing rhetoric riddled in respectability will not save her, and even when disrupting normative forms of discourse through rhetorics of disrespectability, Black women must consistently craft new ways of negotiating and renegotiating their voices and bodies to survive and thrive in a world using their likeness against them. This particular womanist work not only considers this reality but is written through an inscribed lens that theorizes from it and through it.

At present, there are only a few studies from any scholastic field dedicated to Black women politicians. In particular, fewer analyze anything of their speech content and style and the importance of their rhetorical personas from a Black feminist or womanist perspective. Most recently, Anastasia Curwood published *Shirley Chisholm: Champion of Black Feminist Power Politics* (2023) detailing Chisholm's political career and journey as an advocate for women and multicultural coalition building. Similarly, this text presents the rhetorical ingenuity of Chisholm as unique and distinct but differs by not comparing (and at times) contrasting three figures whose personas are held together by a shared bond of bidding for the American presidency. As explained by Ambassador Moseley Braun in an interview with *The Washington Post*, "When you run into the confluence of race and gender it makes it a doubly difficult set of hurdles." And although Chisolm claimed to be a candidate for the office of president of the United States of America, her announcement speech, along with Moseley Braun and Harris, pressed against the weightiness of what their race and gender meant for American voters (Chisholm 1972). Beyond the theoretical implications highlighted throughout this book are the notes of similarities between each candidate, marking how their rhetorical ideals diverge. As such, a creative exchange is built beyond the importance of a single person but as a way to seek the direction toward building space for a wider trajectory of rhetorical thought. Embedded within the analysis of these presidential announcement speeches given by Black women is, in essence, what can be warranted as womanist rhetorical moments of Sankofa and *nommo* in expanded form.

WOMANIST RHETORICAL THEORY AND BLACK WOMEN AS POLITICAL CANDIDATES

In her essay *If the Womanist Rhetoricians Could Speak*, womanist rhetorician Kimberly Johnson (2015) writes, "Systemic racism influences institutional racism, which continues to perpetuate the silencing of our black female scholars in academia" (162). However, I contend that systemic racism also works to silence them within the political arena and/or scholars of political communication. There is no arena for Black women to totally escape from this phenomenon.

Johnson continues by saying, "We [Black women] have to use our own voices, our own experiences, and our own standpoint to voice who we are, what we think, and what we want. We have to utilize our own agency in order to fight for what we want" (162). That is why, in this book, a standpoint centering a Black woman's epistemology and ontology asks several pointed questions that relate to her knowledge and experience of the world, while rhetorically analyzing each speech. What she *knows* to be true and the lens through which she experiences it within her embodied existence, not simply outside of herself, is uniquely critical to womanist work. The questions highlighted in working to understand the rhetor behind the speeches are (1) How does the central rhetor reclaim her voice using the tenet radical subjectivity as a liberative ethic? (2) How does the central rhetor reconstruct discursive space using the tenet of critical engagement to transform conventional communicative definitions? (3) How does the central rhetor reconstitute and reframe her epistemological privilege by accepting the tenet of redemptive self-love? (4) How does the central rhetor reimagine her audience by reforming and renorming a specified polis through traditionally communal cues, codes, and morals? While a polis is arguably different than an audience, these terms are also not mutually exclusive when thinking about Black political communication on a presidential stage. Due to the fact that American voters are actively engaging in the civic discourse of these Black women, in some way, broader parameters and definitions typically assigned to normative prescriptions of political communication must be provided. By asking these kind of questions, the rhetorical analysis within each respective chapter not only works at its best to better perceive a wider scope of the Black woman's experience in the political world she has entered but also works to capture each specific candidate's stance with her respective audience.

As the presidential campaign announcement speeches of Shirley Chisholm, Carol Moseley Braun, and Kamala Harris are measured by a womanist perspective, charting the distinct genius of a Black woman-centered theory in communication is imperative to begin the discussion. Simply defined, womanist rhetorical theory is an ideological and methodological standpoint purposefully grounded in studying the embodied discourse of Black women. As such, this theoretical framework considers the various spaces and places where Black women are the central rhetors and producers of speech acts considering the phenomenological truths permanently inscribed upon their bodies and, by default, their voices. Not only does womanist rhetorical theory begin with sighting and citing Black women as rhetorical agents, but it seeks to analyze how, when, where, and to what extent Black women proactively rename, remember, reclaim, and reimagine discursive space for the survival, wholeness, hope, and fulfillment for themselves over and against heteropatriarchal normative violence in a consumerist, individualist sentimentality oversaturated by neoliberal productivity. To this end, not only does this perspective consider what Black women say and what Black women do, but it also seeks to contend with the moral value of their speech acts and, specific to this text, the political futures they strive to create.

In order to graph this theoretical narrative, I will use chapter 1 as a brief introduction utilizing Wanda Coleman's "Sonnet #61" as a springboard toward capturing the way this theoretical space functions. Similar to scholars in first- and second-wave womanist thought, I argue that Black women's artistic genius through literature, particularly through poetry, narrative, and song, imparts particularly helpful philosophical perceptiveness into the everydayness of their genius. And while it is primarily considered to be a space creatively capturing their expressions of the everyday, I believe it more importantly imparts the ideological insight necessary to stimulate theoretical inquiry into the particular politics that dictate their varied discourse. Coleman captures this by displaying the stark range of options afforded within the grasp of Black women. Put simply, they are given the chance to either build up or tear down new worlds, new possibilities. As it relates to the political sphere, the Black women's announcement speeches studied in this text, as a whole, do this in their own specific manner. Building upon the ideas laid out in the previous section, chapter 2 will squarely define and refine womanist rhetorical theory as a stand-alone discourse. While the goal of this text, womanist rhetorical theory, and the ensuing analysis is not necessarily meant to defend Black women's words, the aim is to value them as their *own*. Displaying their ownership in the midst of racist-sexist-classist political spaces and theoretical milieu is necessary due to the fact that most normative conceptions of nonwhite theoretical undertakings are thought best when presented in a revisionist manner. Instead, this work is presented in a way that builds within and beyond the history of womanist scholarship in order to shape the potential of future womanist communication studies. As such, womanist rhetorical theory stands firmly outside of this archaic manner of building from the margins, or with the master's tools as suggested by Lorde. I end chapter 2 by providing the methodological frame of the previous theoretical insights of womanism by engaging the written vice-presidential announcement speech of political activist Charlotta Amanda Spears Bass. Hers was a speech situated in the particulars of Jim and Jane Crow based on her lived experience and the time in which she was running for political office in this country. As the first Black woman to rise to national prominence by announcing her run for vice-president of the 1952 Progressive Party, her speech serves as a solid example of protowomanist rhetoric and a building block of what I deem womanist prolegomena.

In the chapters that follow, I provide space to highlight each woman and build upon Johnson's ideas for womanist rhetorical criticism within a broader theoretical framework. By using Chisholm's, Moseley Braun's, and Harris's announcement speeches as a revisioning of the presidency and not a revisionist theoretical undertaking, the women's words stand as their own personal creations for political and culture change with them at the helm. Beginning with a brief contextualization to serve as an introduction of the speaker, I will carefully aim to determine how her speech is framed and if her style fits the guidelines of the womanist rhetorical movements as outlined by what I find to be unique protowomanist elements within Bass's speech. Because no one can offer themselves to serve a political career without some sort of professional experience or create a campaign speech for the highest office in American society in a vacuum, the background of each Black woman is important to ponder. By using secondary source material to inform (and in many spaces infer) what may not be explicitly stated in her speech, I will seek the ingenious infusions of rhetorical reactions and movements that would produce a measurable womanist style. While it is not wholly imperative to cast the rhetor as womanist, Black feminist, or otherwise, I do believe it is important to hypothesize a model for womanist sensibilities in the political sphere. This can help broaden communication studies in general and womanist rhetoric in particular by providing space to navigate for future scholarship, candidate strategy, and even how everyday audiences work with and within marginalized audiences beyond a survival rhetorical ethic. Black women's creative exchange and public advocacy do not stop short of the dichotomy of life and death. Womanist rhetorical theory suggests that it is much more complex.

Chapter 3 draws from the concept of womanist rhetorical theory's definition by applying a historical backdrop for Black women's political speeches, specifically at the national level with the first politically pragmatic Black, female presidential candidate, Congresswoman Shirley Chisholm of New York. I argue that Chisholm, standing on the shoulders of countless others, works toward what Watkins-Dickerson and Johnson (2019) have called a womanist rhetorical framework. By thinking again through Johnson's work on womanist rhetorical criticism and social ethicist Stacey Floyd-Thomas's womanist tenets, I analyze the presidential announcement speech of Shirley Chisholm. Her speech builds from Bass but also stands on its own as a foundation and rubric of what many Black women in politics hope to become. Furthermore, her announcement, at its best, demonstrates what womanist speech aims to do when given the opportunity and space.

Following this, chapter 4 emphasizes an impressive continuation of womanist rhetoric's aim in political space adopted by Senator Carol Mosely Braun during her presidential announcement speech at Howard University. Standing upon the shoulders of Chisholm, Moseley Braun presses forward on the political stage hoping to again make history. Her speech, though different in style, delivery, and context to Chisholm's, still contains much of the textual vibrato of Black religious speech. This type of speech style quite often sharply undermines normative concepts of what a polis is and what an audience *does*. Connecting the womanist tenet of traditional communalism to the rhetorical idea of decorum through what I call a "politics of practicality" is an interesting way in which Moseley Braun distinguishes who she is and what her rhetorical persona as a presidential candidate became. By "establishing protocol" through a practical frame and thanking all gathering to support her candidacy, Moseley Braun signifies that the space in which she stands is fundamentally contextualized by the history of Africans in America and the realities they faced, along with the coalitions in which they must join to survive. Beyond this, it is sacred space. Yet, as earlier testified by Chisholm (1970), political agency is one of the most powerful tools to promote change and improvement.

With the trail blazed afire by Chisholm and Moseley Braun, I finally examine the speech of Senator Kamala Harris in chapter 5. Not only is the contextual background of Harris's speech strategically positioned in front of a space that has historically been a place void of the "blind justice" it should stand for, but her commentary is immediately constructed by defining herself. She actively becomes the exemplary first-generation American status as a daughter of hard-working, student-immigrants. Entering into the race at the particular moment that she does is decisive and deliberate, not passive. In some ways, she keeps with a womanist style in her speech, and in others she seems to be building beyond what has been known or what is familiar. In fact, by automatically situating herself outside of the realities of American (read southern) definitions of Jane Crow racist experience, she moves away from historically Black spaces in favor of reclaiming or reimagining what is within her reach. In some ways, this may seem frivolous and pose an insurmountable task; Harris works to own a reality of her specific creation. By standing in front of Oakland City Hall, she suggests that she is in front of history, not the other way around this time. By shaping her speech around what could be missed within this discursive arc, she begins not on the shoulders of a specifically Africana or African American perspective but as a model idea of who is a citizen and who can become president of the United States. By embodying this persona, she becomes an exceptional success story purporting the American dream. Holding tightly to this, her announcement speech somewhat unfolds into the ambiguity of her race and the perception of California's liberal political nature.

Finally, chapter 6 will present additional musings for the future of womanist rhetorical theory beyond political communication and traditional rhetorical analysis. Several women in the field of communication have found value in studying artifacts from a decidedly womanist perspective building on all of those who have lived in a raced-gendered-classed experience in a world where anti-Blackness runs rampant. Black women have not only been leading on the front lines of change but, like Texas congresswoman Jasmine Crockett, have been rhetorically shaping political conversations. These conversations are catapulted by an increase in enhanced technology and access, social media activism, and the persistence of racist-sexist-classist regimes refusing to let Black Lives Matter, or at least *breathe*. While I provide preliminary predictions and recommendations for the use of womanist rhetorical theory inside and outside of the ivory tower, I also consider its accessibility and usability in Black women's political campaigns. Not only is this a very realistic and possible change with eight Black women mayors at the helm of major US cities at the writing of this text, but they are becoming some of the most widely educated individuals and newest entrepreneurs in the country. Thus, access to their speech acts beyond the political sphere is necessary for inquiry, and the ideological trajectory of womanism is not relegated only to Black women in the United States.

Yet because the primary concern of this text centers upon the rhetoric of Black women and the American presidency, the analysis presented will remain dedicated to this setting. With this said, *is* a Black woman for president the balm and remedy to heal and improve the land? The answer to this question may not be expressly available in the study to come, but by foregrounding Black women who dared to be themselves in spaces that often reject them, I argue that there is a motherlode of wisdom to glean. These women came to voice in harsh political spheres while simultaneously hoping to build something better for all those whose faces remain at the bottom of the proverbial wells. At its best, this book theorizes through a womanist framework and aims to analyze the ways in which three Black women built a political persona through their announcement speeches that captured the need, *possibility*, and belief in seeing themselves as a Black woman who could be the president of the United States of America.

Chapter 1

Bringing a Purse to the Political Stage

Introducing Womanist Rhetorical Theory as a Metatheory for Communication Studies

reaching down into my griot bag
of womanish wisdom and wily
social commentary, i come up with bricks
with which to either reconstruct
the past or deconstruct a head. dolor
robs me of art's coin
as i push, for peanuts, to level walls
and rebuild the ruins of my poetic promise. From
the infinite alphabet of afroblues
intertwinings, i cull apocalyptic visions
(the details and lovers entirely real)
and articulate my voyage beyond that
point where self disappears

mis violentas flores negras
these are my slave songs
—"AMERICAN SONNET #61" BY WANDA COLEMAN

The rhetoric Black women create (and are required to respond to) is different because it *has to be*. It is the "but still, like dust, I rise" ethos outlined by poet laureate Maya Angelou ([1978] 2013) matched with the persistent presence of mind and tongue to "fight and struggle toward the light of a better day" as taken up by Charlotta Amanda Spears Bass (Kelly 2020). Steadily striving through and beyond experiences of triple jeopardy and tripartite oppression, it safeguards an unyielding will to *yet* persist, no matter in which pulpit, platform, or public square it finds itself. This book is similar in its scholastic mission taking up the task to study political communication from a distinctly womanist perspective. This is done with the goal of actively disrupting normative rhetorical strategies often upheld as the only viable (read valid or worthwhile) means toward analyzing any text, specifically intellectual conceptions regarding presidential discourse, or otherwise reserved spaces and places defined and outlined traditionally by white men. Who *can* be president is just as contentious of a subject as who *sounds* presidential. As such, the most important place to begin the work concerning the radically different discursive posture Black women take up must begin, not necessarily with their speeches and the political careers that positioned them to take the stage but with the contextual backdrops of their ontological situatedness as Black women in the United States of America. Considering Sonia Sanchez's argument that the poet serves as cultural arbiter for political change and liberative hope, Wanda Coleman's sonnet #61 immediately leads our analysis into a tactical demonstration of the ways in which Black women come to voice. This internalized interrogation of options not only leads well as a conjunction toward conceptualizing the speeches of Black women running for president of the United States of America but also helps us visualize the delicate rhetorical battles they incessantly face. Theirs are battles that in some way, shape, form, or fashion seem to always be met with political struggle and real-world ramifications if not discursively discerned with care.

Taken from her collection of poems *Bathwater Wine*, "Sonnet #61" allows us to witness an intense internal conversation developing from a Black woman re-creating, reimagining, and redefining options for herself and the world she wants to see rebuilt. Pondering the ways in which she endeavors to articulate her deeply held beliefs and perspectives of an anti-Black society dedicated to "take her out," the woman in Coleman's poem postures a strategy for a counterattack while simultaneously cross-examining her surroundings. Claiming a sense of strategic and ontological agency, her rhetorical refusal to be stripped of personhood and instead hold firm to her choice to change the world around her is all held within her reach. However, as captured in the voice and persona of Okoye, general of the Dora Milaje from *Black Panther*, the rebuilding only comes "if she wants to" (Coogler 2018). As explained by bell hooks (1994), "Coming to voice is not just the act of telling one's experience. It is using that telling strategically—to come to voice so that you can also speak freely about other subjects" (148). While this woman "comes to voice" and into her authentic self, Coleman's protagonist begins the radical transformation within to pursue radical transformation without. Brick by brick she builds her theoretical and methodological tools to tear down the everyday towers she must breech in order to see a new reality upon the horizon. However, she begins, not with the philosophically empty pontifications of white capitalist, patriarchal mores of citizenship built within a design of destiny emptily manifesting (read stealing) other people's brilliance, culture, and likeness. She instead commences her task by seeing herself as a valid and valiant rhetorical critic and capable cultural reader. Whether looking to lead a political charge at the highest seat in the country or existing beyond surviving the everyday, Black women's sonnets, songs, symbols, and synopses of the social order dare to turn death-dealing situations into decidedly different outcomes for the communities they serve and love.

A BAG FOR EVERY OCCASION

Beginning with what is in her griot bag, not to be confused with what would usually be considered the frivolity assumed to be within the everyday woman's purse, we venture in to see what she reaches down to grab as the poem moves along, line by line. Women, and as it relates to this specific study, *Black women*, have been known to carry a purse to hold anything (and everything). Not only do purses exist as accessory for any fashion of clothing, but they present the opportunity to fast fit the needs they are called to act upon at a moment's notice. Exhibiting their ability to immediately bargain necessity for form, function, fashion, and/or facility, the Black woman's bag, purse, pocketbook, or satchel serves as metaphorical and literal briefcase carrying concepts to critically call to the carpet heteronormative violence; cleverly yet subversively acquire and acknowledge knowledge of the whispering behind closed doors; draft narratives of escape and a dream of utopia; and persistently possess ready-to-use or build-as-you-go knowhow for various expeditions to change the world for the better. Whether escaping enslavement on the race northward to freedom or accompanying their Sunday's best dress toward the White House, purses carry wallets with money for tithes and transformative justice; lipsticks for last-minute talks and networking sessions; identification cards that get you in and out of *good trouble*; mirrors to look back for the necessary Sankofa moments and look ahead to ensure safety in blind spots; snacks for children under your care which may better serve to ward the scent off as the troupe scurries away; and even building blocks, pens, pencils, laptops, rulers, and drafting paper to draw up blueprints for remedying the world politically, economically, and otherwise.

Some women carry purses everywhere, and some do not. Some women carry big purses, and others carry what could be called small handbags. Either way, every Black woman carries a meaningful metaphorical bag of knowledge that teaches her how to prepare and protect herself as she engages the world around her. Similar to Aretha Franklin, whose policy was to be paid in full *and* in cash before most performances lest the world tries (once again) to "rip her off," when *in their bag*, Black women are making time to get paid their due and in full (Shange 1979, 63). David Remnick explained in a 2018 interview with Jaqueline Weiss, "[Aretha Franklin] collects on the spot or she does not sing. The cash goes into her handbag and the handbag either stays with her security team or goes out onstage and resides, within eyeshot, on the piano" (para 6).

Other Black women, like Shange's *Juanita*, realize they should never allow anyone to "walk off with all of [their] stuff," which was a practical practice placed within everyday reality. It is not about trust but about living through and surviving the "rip-off," or deceit and deception of death-dealing (discursive in this analysis) devices. Whether robbing her financially or stealing the frameworks and words in which she is working to rebuild and reimagine, Black women's purses signify a multiplicity of experiences of the world in very particular ways. As such, before we can begin to break down the political personas of Black women who dared to dream that their voices could carry a nation, Coleman shows us that we must mine the motherlode of their wisdom, wit, words, and the ways they exist and persist in the world with metaphorical (and very real) bags on their shoulders.

Capturing the heavy load Black women have had to carry, the "bag lady" as presented by Erykah Badu also makes us reread and revisit Colman's womanish griot bag beyond the fact that she is going to hurt her back "*dragging all them bags like that.*" Reading beyond what seems to be a simple song or poem allows us to acknowledge what either persona is working to reject though her head is heavy burdened and (seemingly) bowed down by the weight. In many ways, that heaviness is captured within sayings that hold deeper meaning, especially when articulated among women. As explained by Valerie Gray Lee, the language of any people reflects their thoughts, their values, their culture. Instead of using "conventional English" to express their themes, many Black women novelists employ a folk talk that is metaphorical, instructive, and entertaining. Although Black novelists often use "conventional English" to carry the narrative voice in their works, they use folk language to capture the more subtle dynamics of Black life from testifying to signifying (1980, 266).

Passing down epistemic foresight outlined by past experiences, Janie's grandmother implores her, "Honey, de white man is de ruler of everything as fur as Ah been able tuh find out. Maybe it's some place way off in de ocean where de black man is in power but we don't know nothin' but what we see" (Hurston [1965] 2009, 16). Here, Hurston uses Nanny's character to provide explanation in plain text for others what is already understood by Black women. Using this rejoinder, we are able to explore the cue to silently sympathize through culturally gained knowledge and how it frames constant realities and future possibilities. Eventually, Nanny ends by pointing out, "De white man throw down de load and tell de n----r man tuh pick it up. He pick it up because he have to but he don't tote it. He hand it to his womenfolks. De n----r woman is de mule uh de world so fur as Ah can see. Ah been prayin' fuh it tuh be different wid you" (16). Bringing Coleman, Badu, Shange, and Hurston together demonstrates womanist methodological mechanics used to navigate the world around them. Whether through the sentiments of poetry, song, or narrative fiction outlined in folk talk, the necessity to bring forth Black women's words, ways, and wisdom carry from the posturing of the everyday into the political sphere.

Becoming the president of the United States has historically been considered one of the highest honors in the nation. While it certainly involves effort, the intention to work in this space, as articulated through the words of Chisholm, Moseley Braun, and Harris, moves toward rebuilding and recreating something that is decidedly different from traditional considerations of the office. Yet, win or lose, studying Black women's discursive determination to push forth transformational politics in or out of the spotlight from a nontraditional perspective thus commands our academic attention. In order to civically transform the history of American electoral discourse on any level, the very real weight of the griot bag brings forth the blessing and curse of an epistemological privilege of those who are oppressed. These are the ones who are physiologically and psychologically weighed down with the gift of having sight beyond sight. Theirs is an insight that rightfully provides adequate tools to truly consider and conceptualize Shirley Chisolm's, Carol Moseley Braun's, and Kamala Harris's presidential announcement speeches. The work thrust upon them is not simply theirs to keep but, unfortunately, is theirs to carry and is a weight rarely with options to share. Womanist ethicist Katie Canon explains: "Work may be a "moral essential," but Black women are still the last hired to do the work that White men, White women, and men of color refuse to do, and at a wage that men and White women refuse to accept. Black women, placed in jobs that have proven to be detrimental to their health, are doing the most menial, tedious, and by far the most underpaid work, if they manage to get a job at all" (1998, 58).

Similar to the Black women who spoke publicly about their political views elsewhere, they hold within their metaphorical purses either bricks to build or to toss toward selling truths, not haphazardly but wholly with careful cognition and meticulous management. Their work forces the citizenry to contend with their presence as potential leaders. Thus, the emergence of a purse, pocketbook, handbag, or griot bag in Coleman's work also calls into question what these vessels of storage *actually* hold.

Using Coleman's poem as a frame moreover allows us to begin outlining teleological aims of re-creating space for broadening the conversation of Black women in national politics. This frame not only is held within the particular of our experience but is unique to what has been standardized as the norm. This text takes seriously the charting of theoretical space for analyzing Black women's discourse and the context in which it exists; it does so in a manner that must be deliberately and decidedly different than feminist viewpoints, standpoints, and experiences, as these can be strangely laced in the fruits and frivolities of white supremacy. Certainly, for Black folx in general, the power of *life* and *death* are widely held not only within orality but in the ordinariness of the everyday. Purses, poetry, pulpits, podiums, platforms, and pumps are just as political as the American presidency, if not more. This reality is captured in the entirety of Coleman's poem as her analysis moves to understand and explore the use of agentive power to "level walls and rebuild the ruins."

For better (and/or worse) these thoughts of the world that they live in and the ways in which they can destroy it or make it better conjure up concepts, criticisms, and even consequences of acting "too womanish," "feeling oneself," or the uncanny ability to be proud and unapologetic like the late congresswoman Shirley Chisholm. A confidence like this projects pontifications and visionary statements that she is indeed *unbought and unbossed* in a world, in large part, unwelcoming to her. *She does not care.* And yet, through this process, she "comes to voice" or finds the tone, tune, and tenor of the genuine sound within herself. Considering the fact that Black women are always and already marked, Hall submits that "Black (women's) agency is a fugitive act in that as 'speaking subjects' our truth-telling celebrates, performs, and makes visible our refusal to stay in hegemonic frames, confirming our status as a threat to white supremacy. It is a fugitive act because it is an active demonstration of our refusal to stay in the place ascribed for us" (Hall, 343). By using the privilege of her position as a raced-gendered-classed-category in this world to see various perspectives at the same time, she "flips the script" and re-creates better options. Black women, like the women studied in this text, pave a way to reimagine and reconstruct power dynamics with the poise necessary to carry forth the belief that she can push any podium, pulpit, or platform for good as she holds tightly to her metaphorical purse. Carried with all of this is a design mandate to evolve into a person whose eventual actions (or inactions) promote transformation for herself and the ones she loves most. The same happens on the political stage, where Black women form their rhetorical personas differently. Because they are not given the unconscious "benefit of a doubt" when working toward re-creating space for themselves, let alone as civic leaders, their road toward drafting a presidential announcement speech is as unique as the speech itself.

It is speech produced and highlighted by vast expressions of womanhood and femininity denied, though usually respected for others. Also, the theoretical designs necessary to recapture it in each speech to be analyzed in this text flow in a way that acknowledges the points of Canon and Coleman: it is work that must be done, and the decisions are hers alone. As such, choosing three Black women who *dared* to disrupt and dismantle the traditional conceptions and caricatures of the American presidency is *indeed* a fugitive act of signaling death, while also signaling a liberative framework that speaks life into once desolate spaces. Such spaces may have rarely, *if ever*, considered Black women's bodies in this way. Yet the reality of who is in charge and in command is drastically changing, particularly with the 2020 election of President Joseph Biden and Vice-President Kamala Harris. Thus, beyond the study of typical public pontifications and hegemonic performativity from *the patriarchy*, this text argues that there is a great need to study political communication outside of the traditional "good speeches" description.

Theories in Our Bags

Good speeches are typically cast as such through neoclassical/Aristotelian concepts of what rhetoric is and who is capable of being a good and/or effective communicator. Centering this particular methodological frame ties the cannon, students, activists, and wider society to rhetoric's most predictable Greco-Roman foundations in civics. Only dealing with *the* polis having a voice in the public square and cities built upon the hills of liberty studied through normative lenses that leave nothing at the table for Black women and others on the margins, rhetoric studied in this manner leaves much more at hand for those who dare to challenge faith in what is familiar. As such, "Rhetoric's embeddedness in citizenship is so ubiquitous as to be taken for granted, in part because of our preoccupation with the public and political realms. Studies of public address have by and large centered on "great speeches" by politicians and other significant citizens of Western nation-states. As the discipline has considered public discourses more broadly, we have turned attention to the civic practices of ordinary citizens, many of whom demand inclusion in state and national formations in innovative ways" (Chavez 2008, 164). I read Coleman's poem as a manifesto. It is not merely art for art's sake but an orthodox, standardized representation of womanist rhetoric *or* what it should mark its foundations to be.

The analytical form and frame Coleman charted against much of the neo-Aristotelian and postmodern work that uplifts ancient philosophies that for centuries have been building blocks for white hegemonic violence compels us to deal with the fact that there are more conceptually complex, multidimensional, and liberative communication models available. These are ones that begin and end with people who hold experience as a much better teacher than recitation of empty theories that hold promises for a set, limited few. As womanism is the frame held in regard for this text, the argument before us sets up women who dare to be themselves in a world that refuses their embodied voice, thus making it difficult to move within that voice and articulate its full purpose. Womanism, which does not simply begin with the epistemological preferences of Black women but dives directly into how they cultivate and conceptualize those experiences as axiological springboards for *doing* theoretical work, will facilitate the new ways forward in analyzing the speeches and political personas built by Chisholm, Moseley Braun, and Harris while, in turn, creating canonical space for other womanist rhetorical analysis in the future.

Moving between and not beyond the words of Coleman, this text works to define precepts to grasp and frame womanist scholarship in communication as an exercise that is conceptually complex and methodically meticulous. Womanist ethicist Stacey Floyd-Thomas couches Black women's analytical aptitude through the term *critical engagement*. She characterizes the ceaseless intellectual exercise of Black women facing the quotidian habits of surviving white culture similar to the prose of Coleman (1994). In her text *Deeper Shades of Purple: Womanism in Religion and Society*, Floyd-Thomas explains that critical engagement is

> the epistemological privilege of Black women borne of their totalistic experience with the forces of interlocking systems of oppression and

strategic options they devised to undermine them.... 2. an unequivocal belief that Black women hold the standard and normative measure for true liberation; the capacity of Black women to view things in their true relations or relative importance; and while expected to be among the chief arbiters of accountability, advocacy, and authenticity, they, too, must be faithful to the task of expanding their discourse, knowledge, and skills.... 3. a hermeneutical suspicion, cognitive counterbalance, intellectual indictment, and perspectival corrective to those people, ideologies, movements, and institutions that hold a one-dimensional analysis of oppression; an unshakable belief that Black women's survival strategies must entail more than what others have provided as an alternative. (2006, 208)

Unlike the well-received white writers and artists whose lack of formal education can catapult them to heights of glory and great attainment for art and academic purpose, immediately being deemed theoretically deep or influential, Coleman's character rationalizes that the civic and monetary benefits of writing and living through "slave songs" or real-lived experience is simply not enough. These experiences, though creatively curated and intimately incorporated into her stories of *real* personal pain and perseverance are neither socially nor scholastically lucrative. Even as these truths are unearthed by her own embodied familiarity, they can quickly become consumed and commodified by capitalist utilization based on the ever-fixed axiological mission of racist-sexist-classist hegemonic exploits. Far too often, they do. Thus, the astute revelations Black women employ and the futurist visions they can deploy are far too often lost among us or simply cast away as frolicsome because they do not follow the direct order of respectability politics.

The truths they carry and work to articulate are not at all notes half-scattered. Conversely, they are built on the back(s) of a past continuing to survive and subvert monuments of malevolence made beautiful in an America still thriving on the gluttonous consumption of Black and Indigenous bodies. Certainly, our American political history is broadly conceived by ideographs such as Manifest Destiny, which was nationally branded by the late American president James Polk. This and other loosely cast neoimperialistic ideals are embedded in expansionist exploits that see America as a (or the only) utopia for what is conceived to be a free society of opportunity implanted in perpetual promise sold off to the highest bidder. For this reason, reshaping and broadening the conversation of American political communication and presidential rhetoric is how public interaction paves the way for civil progress.

Therefore, before Shirley Chisholm could break the glass ceiling in 1972, Carol Mosely Braun could use her senatorial race as a springboard toward the presidency in 2004, and Kamala Harris could envision herself as a viable candidate in 2020 and eventually took her oath to serve as vice-president of the United States of America during a globally debilitating health pandemic, these women had to poignantly press and prophetically pontificate their right and rite to be seen and heard with dignity and decency beyond where others wanted them to remain. To a great degree, the history of Black women begins at the auction block, and their possibilities are limited within the cultural categories and caricatures that make others comfortable. However, by rhetorically engaging the political options available to Black women, as outlined by Coleman, I argue that being *womanish and wily* is a prerequisite for not merely eventual survival in rhetorical space but living beyond liminal visions of society. It involves catapulting an idea for Black women to be giants with broad shoulders so they can position themselves and others. It attends to the consistent project of projecting these same Black women, and the ones to come along in the future, into political arenas with "griot bags" and "pocketbooks" held tightly by their sides as though they are protecting the possibilities for a whole new world. It is a theory unto itself, going above and beyond a name, while also holding tightly to a critical truth: it is her choice to choose the name, the boundaries, and the possibilities. In spite of the fact the eventual outcome may not fall totally in her favor, she *yet* dared to be herself.

Chapter 2

"Never Ask for Permission to Lead"

Reimagining Presidential Speeches Through Womanist Rhetorical Theory

In a Twitter (before it became X later that year) post dated February 19, 2023, then senator Kamala Harris shared "my message to Black women and girls everywhere: Never ask for permission to lead." As it relates to this text, Harris's advice follows the sentiments of her predecessors. Shirley Chisholm and Carol Moseley Braun were both keenly aware of their double minority status while serving. Chisholm's oft-quoted phrase "If they don't give you a seat at the table, bring in a folding chair" quite possibly speaks beyond what is often assumed to be vague, indirect injustices of misogynoir. Considering the commentary of Pat Schroeder, who was the first congresswoman from Colorado, Chisholm's folding chair axiom addresses the active anti-Black and sexist beliefs, behavior, and practices of their colleagues. Schroeder expressed some of her own challenges from Louisiana representative F. Edward Hebert and his views of women and African Americans during a 2008 NPR interview. On the basis that "African-Americans and women were only worth half a House member in his eyes, he made us (Schroeder and Representative Ron Dellums) share a chair.... That's the environment Shirley was working in" (Schroeder 2008). So, when asked about Black women in politics, it is no surprise that Ambassador Moseley Braun rationalized, "In a time when money is more important than ever in our politics, you take the confluence of those things [race and gender], it's a small wonder why there are not more women, women of color, women who are not from very privileged backgrounds from getting involved" (2014).

Traditionally and historically, politics in the American arena, like the academy, has been a contest fought between educated elites. Chisholm, Moseley Braun, and Harris have verbalized the complexities of service and success in a system dominated and defined by white men. Their leadership style, status, and stance to ensure equality for everyone presents them limited communicative options in the public square, thus presenting an opportunity to reconsider the ways in which we, as scholars, should think about their public speech. Applying a new, and arguably more thorough theoretical, lens can facilitate movement toward better understanding the entire scope of issues their communicative acts signify. Therefore, this book as a whole, and this chapter in particular, takes the recommendation of Vice-President Harris. I center and explore a primarily womanist theoretical lens to study the political communication of Black women as a framework that can be applied within the field of communication but is also useful anywhere Black women are present and/or presented.

While many have studied the extensive résumé of Chisholm and her historical influence and a now growing number of scholars look toward elements of ingenuity in Moseley Braun's and Harris's rhetoric, the quest of this chapter is to solidify another methodological and ideological positionality that better suits their situatedness as Black women in the American sphere. Admittedly, womanism and other theoretical perspectives on the margins have been forced to work from the shadows of scholarship to slowly shift the center. Such work and efforts are typically completed by being coerced to underscore already canonized forms of analysis. It could be worded as "taking an established theory and building on it" or simply incongruent with the canonized discourse. Either way, settling for watered-down theory and citing the long list of white, primarily male scholars who have laid the "appropriate" groundwork in the field does nothing to disrupt or reframe the cannon. It instead discards the meaty insightfulness of everyday folx as practical wisdom, not canonized theory. First- and second-wave womanism (and Black feminism) have done this work with righteous indignation; however, the following considerations do not. Inside and outside of the scholastic cannon, Black women are not always considered credible cultural critics, even when in defense of themselves and their own communities. However, Black women, when speaking truth into a world where platforms, pulpits, and podiums are not always welcoming to Black women, leading without permission is in the job description. Black women *do* the business of work that *builds* Black women and their communities. This is work that is deep, thought provoking, intellectually weighty, and mentally strenuous but always wholly soul-fulfilling work with endless rewards that build wells that never run dry. Not only is the intention of this chapter to work toward unpacking a working definition of womanist rhetorical theory, but the hope is also to provide a new way for *how* scholars, readers, activists, dreamers, and thinkers should implement or understand an unapologetically womanist identity. Highlighting Black women, not merely as subject for study but as expert behind the pen of the theory itself is paramount to pushing the canonical norm.

To be clear, womanist rhetorical theory, of course, is a theory anyone can use, but it is not a perspective, experience, or wisdom everyone can have. To understand, perceive, or rightly/righteously deploy womanist sensibilities is something altogether special, exclusive, unique, and at times riddled with the pain of historical hardship between striving and thriving. While I argue womanist theory as a metatheory, and that a womanist rhetorical theory for communication studies can extend beyond the traditionally held conventions of (white) feminist and Black feminist theories of research, it is not a monolithic categorization all Black women must accept or employ. At the same time, *most* if not *all* Black women experience some sort of effect and affect of misogynoir whether they acknowledge this truth or hide it beneath of series of other everyday microaggressions. These microaggressions, far too often, coerce them to find a place between surviving and thriving in a world that views discursive liberation for the marginalized as antithetical to the human condition because such an ideal is constructed through and by a very narrow white heteronormative, Western perspective. Moreover, womanism at its simplest ideological location should not be captured merely under a classification or kind of "feminism," as it is often cast in various classrooms purporting study of worldwide, transnational/international or multiple feminist perspectives and categories. This is not only a false depiction of intersectionality but the history three decades of scholarly publications in womanism and generations of organically passed collective wisdom has lived and levied several generations through trial and tribulation. It has been passed down into the hearts, culture, kitchens, politics, and genius of countless Black women seeking to find and celebrate their voices and those of their foremothers (Watkins-Dickerson 2022, 202). Womanist thought carries with it the holistic voice, feeling, emotion, concern, vigor, and spirit of Black women, while centering their worldview and uplifting verbiage that is uniquely theirs, and theirs alone. It also crucially favors an ethical mandate striving toward the liberation of Black people across the diaspora and those incapable of obliterating the marginality they experience by the ways in which whiteness silences their voices and realities.

To do this work, this text offers a definition of womanist rhetorical theory and its efficacy for researching Black women rhetors in the field of communication by using the presidential announcement speeches of Black women as texts for critical, practical, and theoretical analysis. Taking a decidedly multidisciplinary approach to build this work allows space to holistically center Black women's theoretical voice in communication and complementary disciplines. Finally, moving beyond theory to describe the methodological possibilities for doing womanist work in rhetorical theory, I outline a style guide for the speeches in order to determine whether they are womanist in their sentiments, Black feminist in their scope, a mixture of the two theoretical ideals, or something else altogether. The tone of these ideas is set against the protowomanist rhetoric of Charlotta Amanda Spears Bass. By centering the idea of the race woman and Alston's "womanish ways," a close reading of the vice-presidential nomination acceptance speech of Bass given in Chicago, Illinois, at the National Convention of the Progressive Party displays a working standard for reading and analyzing womanist rhetoric. Like Coleman's protagonist, Bass's political persona during the speech and in her everyday undertakings takes up bricks to build new worlds of possibility for herself and her community. Understanding what her words can mean and/or provide for the political rhetors in this examination of Black women as American presidential candidates will make plain the vision of what womanist rhetorical theory has already been defined to be in earlier works but also how it practically unfolds in public discourse. After considering Bass, the text moves into the subsequent presidential announcement speeches, reimagining future works in womanist theories of communication.

TOWARD DEFINITIONS: WHAT IS WOMANIST RHETORICAL THEORY?

To begin, womanism views whiteness itself as a fundamental problem to the goal of true equity and equality for all marginalized peoples, not merely reduced to rejecting "the patriarchy." Like the bricks held within Coleman's griot bag, womanism has typically held with it a sensibility that has historically considered deconstructionist theoretical visions against heteropatriarchal normative whiteness frivolous, yet necessary, particularly in its first wave. However, in second- and third-wave womanism, visions that busy our projects with revisionist goals not only take our eye away from the prize but keep us from the shaping and living into the theoretical manifestations that will create future realities for thriving. Thus, womanist rhetorical theory builds itself differently and pushes against and through and beyond the normative grain. It cannot and does not find protections through gendered, raced, and/or class stratifications in the ways available to men of color specifically, white women in particular, and people of color (POC) more broadly. Black women, instead, as practitioners of scholarship, political figures, and everyday civilians, find themselves split between the crossroads of a tenuous history. In what some capture under a frolicsome umbrella of feminisms, their very ontological posture in a society that experiences them in a specified manner still goes beyond the goodness and the glory of a short-sighted purview of otherwise phenomenologically dense connective tissue. As such, womanist activists, scholars, preachers, leaders, artists, and adherents of this Black woman positive theoretical framework own their own plot of land, lay their own foundations, and build their own houses bit by bit and brick by brick. Like Haggar, the only biblical figure to name God for herself, Black women claim that in their affliction, God, the universe, or all that is good and right and just, finds her, knows her, and El Roi is indeed "the God who sees." This is a God captured in the reality of the *imago dei*. She is found in herself, and she loves her *fiercely* and without compromise (Shange 1972). In *Sisters in the Wilderness*, Delores Williams picks apart this point through her own exegetical work of Haggar as an enslaved woman bound to patriarchy and obligations of culture and still given agentive voice by a higher power that works to eventually transcend beyond context and culture and convenience. Normative analogies of the wilderness are typically read as restrictive and repressive, yet Williams demonstrates that it can be a space that is liberative and limitless.

From here and elsewhere in the cannon of collective Black women's understanding of the world, a womanist vision, theory, and strategy do not see the wilderness as a place to be defined only by exile and death. It is instead a space where infinite possibilities abound to refresh and reenergize Black women on the journey ahead with an understanding that the option of "going back" or "turning around" surely leads to death-dealing demise, even in the guise of easy compromise. These women, like Harriet Tubman, decide, declare, and decree, "Mama, I'm walking to Canada and I'm taking you and a bunch of other slaves with me" and *indeed* "It wouldn't be the first time" (Floyd-Thomas 2006, 20). These are Black women who understand many more minds and bodies could have been freed, if they only knew they were caged into oblivion and filled with beautiful songs waiting to be sung. More importantly, the key is that when these songs are written, spoken, shared, and arranged, the Black woman's voice brings forth an unrivaled vision for justice and piety and potential and liberation that rings beyond any city's hill.

Far too long, under the guise of an always welcoming, equitable, and diverse discipline of communication, concepts of theory and political communication leave Black women away from the table. Whether the scholars distinguish theory through dense philosophical language or what the late Black liberation theologian James Hal Cone called "intellectual naval gazing," grounding works in communication studies typically refuse to cite Black women as theorists, along with other marginalized groups and individuals. Yet it is clear that Black folx are a race for theory and if it were a footrace the clear intellectual ingenuity and flexibility necessary to survive (and hope needed to thrive) in spite of driving while Black, remaining prepared for the sudden cultural and verbal code switch at work, and striving cannot be lost in the busyness of the everyday. Certainly, Chisholm, Moseley Braun, Harris, and countless other Black women have found their voices challenged, no matter what cultural, social, political, and professional spheres they walk within, into, and strive to move beyond from day to day. Black feminist sociologist Patricia Hill Collins (1998) states, "It is not that elites produce theory while everyone else produces mere thought. Rather, elites possess the power to legitimate knowledge that they define as theory as being universal, normative, and ideal" (xiii). Stacey Floyd-Thomas (2014) gives a similar critique in her essay "The Faith We Love and the Facts We Abhor: A Response to Lisa Sowle Cahill's 'Catholic Feminists and Traditions: Renewal, Reinvention, Replacement.'" In it, she ponders how and why Reinhold Niebuhr achieved great public and scholarly success with his social ethic of pragmatic socialism, in spite of the fact that he never earned a doctoral degree in the field of ethics or elsewhere. She posits, "Was it the white heteropatriarchal privilege of this white scholar-activist that gave him the moral agency and the cultural capital to achieve the success that he had?" (203).

A similar question can be posed to the communication community's enthrallment and sentimentalization of Kenneth Burke (1969), among countless others. The working mission to exclusively rely on revisionist means to add to the cannon directly disregards African philosophical designs that were impressed within and alongside the long upheld and regarded Greco-Roman "ideas" of what rhetoric is and who can define it. Certainly, the quest toward womanist rhetorical theory challenges this in order to build *truly* equitable space for analyzing Black women in political spaces and private places. Hence, Floyd-Thomas finishes her essay by calling for more critical inquiry by stating, "This is not a rhetorical question" and submits that readers must consider the deeper meaning of ethics and the production of scholarship by and for persons on the margins, even though they are not credited with similar celebration for their work in comparison to their white, male counterparts (2006, 58). While Collins and Floyd-Thomas are not producing work within the field of communication, their assessments articulate a problem steadily highlighted across various disciplines. Therefore, we, as contributors and subscribers to the scholarly cannons of our specific fields, must reconsider what voices and bodies are being centered; reimagine who can speak about and shape what should be analyzed as serious and erudite; and renegotiate space to claim who is capable of theorizing within a discipline, or when this practice is initiated and negotiated, at minimum. For this reason, I argue that defining womanist rhetorical theory is a crucial task for moving forward in contemporary musings about how Black women come to voice, politically and otherwise. Yet in order to understand how this field must be shaped, "calling the roll" of Black women scholars who have used womanist considerations and ideologies in their work will help us frame the ways in which we can decipher the speeches of Chisholm, Moseley Braun, and Harris to build this framework for present and future study.

Womanist Prolegomena

Early womanist scholarship draws from Alice Walker's use of the term in "Coming Apart" ([1979] 2006) and formal definition after the publication of *In Search of Our Mother's Gardens* (1983). For years and beyond specific words, Black women scholars have been crafting their own ways of arguing the particularities of Black femininity, womanhood, motherhood, being wives, negotiating their dignity, personhood, citizenship, and humanity all while this is rarely consulted for, challenged for, or denied to white women. Because of this, Black women's ways of escape in a world ripe to deny them space for self-care, positive identity formation, or space for escape, finding artifacts and mediums where such visions of voicing who they are by their own terms is imperative to note and explore. Janice Hamlet's (2000) *Assessing Womanist Thought: The Rhetoric of Susan L. Taylor* was the first published instance in which a Black woman communication scholar introduced the term to the field and found ways Black women crafted alternative spaces for self-love and self-care in widely accessible ways. Citing the work of sociologist Deborah King (1988), Hamlet explains, "The emergence and development of a womanist epistemology and methodology presents African American women and the scholarship about them as distinct subjects of the human family worthy of acknowledgment and study" (2000, 421). Hamlet's use of a womanist epistemology is invaluable, not simply for building womanist rhetorical theory as a conceptual framework but also for providing an axiological and praxeological foundation for doing the work Black women's souls seek after in a discipline wrought with the celebration of white- and male-dominated hegemonic frames from which we typically must pull.

Looking at the outline and scope of *Essence* magazine, a publication historically centering Black women's beauty, fashion, and culture and dedicated to their strivings, Hamlet identifies "seven interrelated themes in editor Susan Taylor's columns: (1) spirit power; (2) harmony and balance; (3) self-affirmation; (4) cultural history and ancestral reverence; (5) love; (6) collective power; and (7) self-destruction" (2000, 424–25). She argues that, as editor, Taylor unites African American women's sharing of a similar spiritual base as a way in which womanist musings are tactically positioned throughout the magazine. This is specifically tied to her position and the columns specifically penned by her, which cast a specific vision of how Black women are portrayed and the information they would find valuable for their reading and pleasure. Hamlet further states, "Through the use of self-affirming language, which communicates a 'can-do spirit,' Taylor teaches African American women how to rely on their own power, the power of their deep-seated and cosmic spirituality and the power that comes from the ultimate unshakable inner knowledge of their own value and talent" (427). Beyond this, Hamlet's use of the term *womanist* to conduct her study notes an important theoretical shift she makes for Black women scholars in communication. By not choosing a plainly feminist, or even a Black feminist, lens, she pushes against conventional standpoints of inquiry effectively and affectively renegotiating space for Black women's ideological giftings to be synthesized in the discipline. As a result, scholars are introduced to the value of drawing from womanism using Hamlet's work as a backdrop for understanding another way to analyze how Black women communicate. This centering of womanist language actively demonstrates how Black women renegotiate relationships inside and outside of the Black community, not simply among themselves. Hamlet's choice to use a lifestyle magazine, typically seen as entertainment in most circles, is a vital and refreshing look at how Black women seek refuge in alternative spaces. By theorizing in a medium celebrating self-reflection, pleasure, and relaxation, Hamlet, Taylor, and even the readers knowingly or unknowingly, willingly and unwillingly, demonstrate Black women having fun, enjoying leisure, and seeking fulfillment in their own circles as an act of political resistance. This resistance is rhetorical and produces knowledge and knowledge-making material only available in a magazine like *Essence*. It also shows how a Black female audience is created. Culturally relevant hospitality along with food for thought and for the soul is provided at an open table for all who are *on one accord*.

Far too often, African American women's theories and critiques against racist, sexist, classist society's use of their backs as bridges fall on unwilling ears, rarely give them credit for their efforts, while co-opting their genius with nary a footnote. While Hamlet is the first Black woman communication scholar to publish her work outlining a womanist epistemology in her rhetorical analysis, there are a list of other women who continue to provide bricks to do the emancipatory work of centering the self as rhetorical critic. This is in line with Brenda Allen's (2002) words from "Goals for Emancipatory Communication Research on Black Women": "Researchers should identify Black women's communicative skills and strategies, including acts of resistance. We should discover how Black women presently and previously use(d) communication not only to cope but also to flourish" (26). In so doing, womanist rhetorical theory is built by using our own cultural capital to contour the conceptual outline and cast visions for a discursive future that liberates, shifts, and creates space for others to be seen in political leadership and otherwise. Although we know of the "Joe and the hoe" jokes (or even the ways we are empathetic and agitated by calls to "lock her up" because of "her e-mails"), we bear witness and hold our breaths right along with then senator Harris in her speech accepting the vice-presidential nomination on August 19, 2020. Wading through the vicissitudes of misogynoir in her wake, whether from a purely Afrocentric cosmological center or not, Black women's bodies, if visible when coming to voice, are not always allowed to hold the tenor of theory that their lives fashion and flourish in from day to day.

Olga Davis provides another crucial underpinning of shaping an effective bibliography and historiography of theorizing through a lens decidedly set by Black women. Whereas her 1999 essay "In the Kitchen: Transforming the Academy Through Safe Spaces of Resistance" highlights the ordinariness of Black women's everyday subversive genius from enslavement onward, her essay "A Black Woman as Rhetorical Critic: Validating Self and Violating the Space of Otherness" (1998) works to center Black women's lived experience and ability to speak on the ways in which society suppresses and oppresses and represses their voices by problematizing their embodied truth-telling. Davis explains that there is a need for work that "advance[s] the need to validate self as a rhetorical critic in order to rediscover Black women's rhetorical tradition" (77). By highlighting and subverting the notion that research must be objectively cast by a nonbodied, disconnected other, a womanist appraisal deems that objectivity is the biggest lie buttressing the ivory tower. Research is not bias-free, nor is there room for it to be inherently impartial. Based on the condition of today's world, I would contend that this is particularly impossible and improbable from a white, male perspective that either has the *potential* to enjoy the benefits of whiteness or readily relaxes within the bounds of capitalist domination.

As Davis posits, African American women's rhetorical tradition and the centering of their ontological, experiential, and epistemological rhetoric is imperative to grasp if we are to push the cannon further and do the work of scholarship. The ever-growing neoliberal touchpoint of "adding Black women and stir" only casts visions of global feminisms that usurp intersectionality as its own; grows faint, frail, and too forgetful to cite Kimberlé Crenshaw; and eventually casts Black women to the bottom of the well where their bodies and voices are disassembled and the usable parts oddly attached to a Grace Jones flashback campaign that "breaks the internet." Davis notes there are plenty of studies regarding the history of Black women's lives and their public discourse, but there is truly a need for defining them as rhetorically savvy and capable of intellectual fervor as it relates to rhetorical theory. She further suggests that when Black women can self-validate their particular experiences at the crossroads of race, gender, and class, we will be able to not only broaden their understanding but also widen the scope of rhetorical study and meaning making they create. This does not come by framing opinions, musings, and real wisdom in the tongue, guise, or theoretical frame of dominant discursive patterns only but also by working from the philosophical and spiritual wisdom of Black women as viable rhetorical critics and adroit cultural readers of the world around them. Therefore, this text bobs and weaves with bricks and blueprints and a little Blue Magic™ to quell white supremacist strongholds and claim space for Black women by writing the self, *myself*, into the theoretical frame. And some cultural connections will follow a pattern of rhetorical refusal, or a slippin' and slidin' in and out of frame, to alleviate any normative comprehension constraints or needs to alleviate white fragility. What is understood need not be explained, and as Auntie Tab says, dats *my business*.

"BRICK BY BRICK": THE MAKINGS OF A WOMANIST RHETORICAL THEORY

Traveling along an uphill battle to get her message across to the masses, each Black woman presidential candidate to be studied in this text is not only fighting in a political ring but also fighting to be heard. As her slogan "fighting Shirley Chisholm" denotes, the late congresswoman Shirley Chisholm had a war on all fronts. Speaking out against the war in Vietnam; creating civil rights legislation on behalf of women and the Black community;

supporting education reform, indigenous rights, and more, she and other Black women in politics consistently make it their business to use their political platform to uplift oppressed communities. These communities, whether raced, classed, gendered, or otherwise categorized as caricature and rhetorical conjecture must fight against the policies of a political machine continuing to undermine their individual agency and personhood, even as tax-paying citizens of the republic.

Davis (1998) writes through a framework to study what she calls a "rhetoric of survival," which I glean to be a space in which Black women find themselves for themselves but must also theorize beyond (77). In bodies triply oppressed by the plight of racism, sexism, and classism, on all accounts, society says they should be incapable of committing to a plan, let alone a discursive blueprint, that facilitates space for reframing their narrative and moving beyond the rhetorical constraints they encounter. Thus, tripartite oppression not only presents social stipulations on the way in which they encounter the world but also frames the way they encroach political campaigns and other means of work. Davis (1998) stresses that "the paucity of rhetorical scholarship on African American women's epistemology and ontology implies that Black women's discursive and nondiscursive practices are inconsequential to understanding human communication..." (77). First- and second-wave womanist scholars in several disciplines have attended to this issue at length but third-wave womanist scholars are dedicated to thinking beyond methods of showing Black women's survival ethics and instead highlighting their hopes, dreams, and reimagined futures.

Davis writes, "The legacy of the kitchen is a rhetorical strategy for negotiating the *outrage* of discrimination, inferiority, and most importantly, white superiority" (1999, 369). Davis outlines the way in which the kitchen or kitchen settings have been a space where Black women have redefined and reenvisioned rhetorical space, praxis, and their ongoing commitment to articulate their experiences through tripartite oppression. Davis's analogy of the kitchen—and the way in which its historical standpoint in slavery was both stagnant and uniquely positioned in a way for cultural discursive retentions to be passed down—is a fresh way to consider African American women's rhetorical trajectory and the struggles she explains they *yet* endure in the academy. She states, "African American women intellectuals have a *place* but not an *importance* in academe. While African American women intellectuals in universities are given academic *homes* from which to, theoretically, obtain mentoring, collaboration, collegiality, and a supportive climate, they are often told—by tenure committees and journal editors—that their work and their very existence is of no importance" (1999, 371).

In *Centering Ourselves: African American Feminist and Womanist Studies of Discourse,* Houston and Davis (2002) build a foundation through utilizing a radical hybrid methodological focus on Black feminist and womanist rhetorical theory in order to center their study on the experiences of Black women, as opposed to using traditional means of rhetorical analysis. In so doing, they illuminate the difference, similarities, and overall mission of an African American women's rhetorical framework from Black feminist and womanist standpoints. Monika Alston extends this consideration in her presentation "'Introducing Womanish Ways': An Invitation to Consider Race and Gender" at the National Communication Association Conference.

Alston (2007) provides a study of Shirley Chisholm, whose radically subjective charisma followed her for an entire career that was dominated by white men saying she did not belong and Black men stating she should wait her turn. Shirley Chisolm's rhetoric was atypical for her time and space in political rhetoric. She did not conduct "business as usual," which is framed by her communicative style to the way in which she campaigned. Alston's presentation provides a guide to how "womanish" ways can be considered in approaching race and gender in politics. She outlines how womanish ways parallel womanist scholarship's four tenets of radical subjectivity, critical engagement, traditional communalism, and redemptive self-love. Her conference presentation is useful in trying to define and explore a womanist rhetorical style that also works within the images produced by the media and the stereotypes that many Black women are forced within despite their position as political figures.

Communication scholar Deborah Atwater (2009) begins this quest toward understanding the rhetoric of Black women in her text *African American Women's Rhetoric: The Search for Dignity, Personhood, and Honor* by analyzing various speech acts. She considers the rhetoric produced from enslavement/slave narratives to media portrayals of former secretary of state Condoleezza Rice. Atwater explains the difficulties of constructing a strategy to communicate in the public sphere and theorizes about Black women's particular rhetorical situation. Following Atwater's ideas of personhood denied, rhetoric and composition scholar Corretta Pittman's (2007) article "Black Women Writers and the Trouble with Ethos" also furthers the discussion about the challenges of establishing credibility as a rhetor. Pittman considers how Harriet Jacobs, Billie Holiday, and Sister Soulja negotiated their agency and worked to establish themselves as credible, trustworthy rhetors as they navigated the confines of enslavement, Jim/Jane Crow, and the modern conception of a post-racial/racist/sexist/misogynist society. Nonetheless, neither Atwater nor Pittman claims a womanist standpoint, and they do not define womanist rhetorical theory or its practical use in the field. What is clear is that their work squarely focuses on the difficulties Black women experience based on their race, class, and gender but also the ways they must overcome these categories to come to voice in the public sphere, to liberate themselves and their community.

In Karen Foss's 2012 entry in the *Encyclopedia of Communication Theory*, she writes, "Rhetorical theory is the body of thought about human symbol use" (1). Drawing from Lloyd Bitzer's (1992) concept of the rhetorical situation, she explains that "rhetoric occurs in response to an exigence or some kind of urgency, problem, or something not as it should be" (1). She continues to explain that the audience is also a major characteristic positively or negatively affecting an exigence in some way. Thus, "rhetoric comes into being, then, when a rhetor observes or creates an exigence and offers discourse designed to bring the interests of the audience to bear on it" (1). Foss continues the entry by discussing the history of rhetoric from Aristotle's conception of it as artful persuasion to contemporary studies, including outsider position theories that not only challenge normative prescriptions of discourse but force it to expand beyond traditional ways of theorizing about communication. Nevertheless, her definition of rhetorical theory is still somewhat sparse for the complex challenges marginalized persons experience, and in particular the multiple jeopardies and multiple consciousnesses embodied in the discourse of Black women (King 1988).

While Foss mentions queer movements, Native and Eastern philosophical understandings, African American, and explicitly feminist techniques, she does not incorporate them fully into her definition, nor does she broadly cite theorists from these theoretical standpoints. POC do have similar experiences, but this does not mean the depth and extent of the violence their bodies must carry is the same. Whereas womanist theory does not seek a targeted entry into what many call the "oppression Olympics," we, as Black women, seeking to come to voice and stretch beyond the static positions society deems for us to stand within differ in the complexities of our struggle. Moreover, while feminism *should be* for everybody, the feminist movement was born and bred in the bed of whiteness. In many ways, this can not only breed and a brand a badge of toxic hegemonic femininity often suppressing and ignoring certain violence(s) that women of color have experienced, in particular but also removes any requirement for full solidarity. To take this a step further, many times this happens at the hands of the very women who call themselves feminists and allies for *the cause*. Despite their sexuality, political position, educational attainment, class affiliation, or even religious beliefs, Black women have to be brave without individual or collective agency and support. Thus, terming this theoretical imperative "womanist" is also a revolutionary act of naming the self and charting space for critical thought.

This is not to say Foss's work of defining what constitutes rhetorical theory does not serve as a starting point to facilitate broader discussion, but this definition does not capture the complexity of Black women's experience. This definition of rhetorical theory, in and of itself, produces a particular constraint for those rhetors on the margins, which must conceive hypotheses, construct discourse, and come to voice in certain situations and in front of skeptical audiences daily. This evidences the rhetorical condition (Asante and Atwater 1986) or the imposition of whiteness (as riteness, righteousness, and rightness) upon bodies that do not fit into the traditional binaries of white hegemonic masculinity in a Western cultural, political, and linguistically confined context. Asante and Atwater define the rhetorical condition as the structure and power pattern assumed or imposed during a rhetorical situation by the communicators. Although the condition may be negotiated by the communicators, different rhetorical situations produce different conditions because the inherent power relationships change from situation to situation. We are not speaking about traditional structural concerns of discourse (i.e., arrangement and style); these follow almost naturally from the structure of the discourse as discourse. What we are arguing is the existence of a rhetoric of structure, not in the sense of a rhetoric about structure but rather a rhetoric of form about the rhetoric of words (Asante and Atwater 1986, 171).

In theory and in practice, Foss's definition imposes a rhetorical condition upon the definition of rhetorical theory by only scantily acknowledging other perspectives. Even though this may not be the intention, there is still a rhetorical limit imposed upon what theory is within the discipline, as only white scholars are listed and considered, effectively e-racing the discussion. In a University of Minnesota Press *Critical Ethnic Studies* blog, an April 2015 entry considers the words of critical cultural theorist Sara Ahmed. It states that Ahmed considers citation (practices) a "rather successful reproductive technology, a way of reproducing the world around certain bodies" (Ahmed 2013, para 3). As such, the blog editors quote Ahmed in saying, "the reproduction of a discipline can be the reproduction of these techniques of selection, ways of making certain bodies and thematics [and voices] core to the discipline, and others not even part" while also challenging readers to consider who they cite and who is silenced (para 4).

Foss, Aristotle, Bitzer, and even the addition of Asante and Atwater's rhetorical condition facilitates the notion that humans perpetually make symbols, both verbal and nonverbal. Some of these symbols are rendered invisible and silent, while others are excavated with great detail and preciseness. Due to this, it is necessary to hypothesize within a framework using a rubric that illuminates and celebrates the vantage point of those human beings who have been permanently cast and castigated as symbols themselves. In this breath and absence, womanist rhetorical theory re-creates podiums and pulpits and platforms to stress the manner a politics of exclusion demonizes othered bodies. Even though rhetors were shaped in the democratic process of the Ancient Greek polis and adapted in American political practice, this is not the case for all, let alone the *sister citizen* in consideration of sociologist Melissa Harris-Perry's (2011) analysis of Black women in the midst of public tragedy. Those persons, typically surviving on the margins of society, have been drafted and designed to signify deviance outside of the predetermined binaries of whiteness, while simultaneously being required to adapt within an exact definition of performing gender and sexuality.

Womanist Rhetorical Theory Is . . .

Womanist rhetorical theory is produced from a specific set of rhetorical conditions that enforce a particularly unyielding, unavoidable rhetorical situation because Black women are subjected to some of the direst positions. While forced to be productive for the consumption and credit of others, their voices are often villainized when, like Mrs. Sophia, they speak their truths, and/or their discursive presence in public manifestos is sidelined to the great man theory like the late Reverend Prathia Hall. In her essay "Mules of the World, Unite: The Feminine Black Atlantic of Zora Neale Hurston" Elsa Charléty (2017) reminds us that within the pages of *Their Eyes Were Watching God* ([1965] 2009), "Zora Neale Hurston states that black women are the mules of the world: they carry the load that white men, white women and black men refuse to carry; they do the work no one wants to do, without praise or thanks" (1). Not only are Black women doing the work, taking a contingency with them to freedom, and the majority of the legwork toward justice, they are left to carry the weight of being doubly oppressed in a society that, according to many, still is not entirely free or providing justice for all.

As consistently argued throughout womanist and Black feminist scholarship, Black women experience the death-dealing despair and destruction of tripartite oppression inflicted by racism, classism, and sexism due to American chattel slavery and global dominance over and against all women, especially those of African descent. Instead of being the product to be consumed by the capitalistic production of misogyny permanently embedded in whiteness, womanist rhetorical theory studies how Black women are themselves production managers for transformative change (Hudson-Weems 1989). This must commence with a praxeological mission to "lay hands" onto the spaces and places and stories and testimonies that have not been told, or those seemingly unreal. They do this by adopting, not adapting, nor appropriating, the four womanist tenets as outlined by womanist religious scholars from Alice Walker's four-part definition of womanism: (1) radical subjectivity, (2) critical engagement, (3) traditional communalism, and (4) redemptive self-love. Doing womanist rhetorical theory necessitates a logically radical spirit that subjects a hermeneutic of suspicion upon normative truth claims, innately possesses an epistemological wisdom producing a critically engaging challenge upon the metaphysical structures of whiteness, is inspired by a traditionally communal love of the folk steeped in a shared ontological situation of Blackness, and strives toward an axiological mission determined to be redemptively self-affirming and self-loving, in spite of all odds. Womanist theory, as a metatheory, begins in the hearts, homes, and hopes of Black women. It is bolstered by an understanding that injustice is not a necessity and that liberative spaces must be created for all, no matter the conventionally canonized rules, regulations, and relegations.

In a more direct way, looking critically at Chisholm's historic run, and the women that have followed, it is a constantly *moving* theoretical framework that pushes beyond typical and traditional rhetorical considerations. This, I argue, was due to the phenomenological history of categorizing Blackness as nonbeing through the invention of chattel slavery and the political economy of whiteness, which leaves Black men and white women captured through the tokenization of their male bodies or white skin. But it extends beyond this structure and builds its own house of rules all the same. It makes meaning from Black women's lived experiences that are narrated by the bodies they survive in and find ways to thrive beyond. While inherently prophetic, womanist rhetorical theory also finds balance, poise, and a sense of order in its centering of the body as a source of knowledge, meaning making, and theory itself.

Discovering both a permanent and philosophical space for womanist rhetorical theory evolves from Michael Leff's 1987 paper "The Habitation of Rhetoric" and his discussion of decorum. Leff writes: "Decorum is the term that best describes the process of mediation and balance connected with qualitative judgment. It is the principle of decorum that allows us to comprehend a situation as a whole, to locate its meaning within a context, and to translate this understanding into a discursive form that becomes an incentive to action. As it applies to the rhetorical act, decorum orders the elements of a discourse and rounds them out into a coherent product relative to the occasion" (5).

While this is true, in its purest form, Leff's consideration only goes so far for the womanist rhetor. The Black woman not only must understand the nature of occupying a pulpit, podium, or political platform, but she must also be able to transform the discursive space to fit her various audience members. And more than this, the nature of studying three Black women on the road to the presidency through their campaign announcement speeches, helps us understand why they *must* use extreme wit and wisdom as they chart forth and craft out new spaces to speak and be heard. Coleman's poem at the heading of this chapter demonstrates that Black women must actively re-create, redefine, reimagine, and reclaim space, place, time, thought, deeds, and more to elucidate their authority and ability to effectively push their audience toward greater heights when she says, "i come up with bricks/with which to either reconstruct/the past or deconstruct a head" (Coleman 1988). With this in mind, womanist rhetors craft their speeches considering the traditional charges of decorum, which are order, etiquette, decency, and relevance to an audience. Yet, when prophetic space needs to be made, the bricks can be directed to deconstruct through a disruptive rhetorical ethic, as well. Therefore, when considering this persuasive perspective, the push for womanist rhetorical theory moves outside of common decorum, extending beyond the metaphysical language and discursive entrapments of the epistemic argument.

By this same token, literary theorist Barbara Christian's (1987) "The Race for Theory" helps us consider Black women's and Black men's words have always been both *rational* and *relational*, keen to upholding and creating *knowledge*, while also being informed by a *critical suspicion* of the world around them, which could simply be defined as common sense. In many ways, Christian writes of her tiring of theory being superimposed upon groups outside of the "center" and the way in which the dominant discourse studies those on the "periphery" (56). She states, "I am particularly perturbed by the movement to exalt theory, as well, because of my own adult history. I was an active member of the Black Arts Movement of the sixties and know how dangerous theory can become" (1987, 50). Even though she criticizes the prescriptive nature of some of the Black Arts Movement theory, her reasoning is underlined by the male-centric voice that extended from this time period and its silencing of Black women's voices and works. To be clear, Christian, along with Gwendolyn Brooks, Beverly Ann Teer, and Sonia Sanchez, among other Black women, were active in not only producing various forms of spoken and written art but were also influential in establishing Black feminist and womanist foundational space. Thus, the critique here is not that theory, in and of itself, has not the ability to be productive and proactive, but in order to enhance the lives of Black women it must be active and rooted in practice or extending a praxeological mission. A necessary "laying on of hands" necessary negates the stagnation that only decorum's proper proscriptions deliver. Thus, it is fluid and functional, prophetic and practical, as well as spiritually inspired and spatially intelligent and aware.

To help with this, Brittney Cooper (2017) explains: "Where embodied rhetoric refers primarily to speech acts, embodied discourse expands to include black women's use of black bodies and corporeal images within both written and spoken texts to advocate for racial and gender equality. Embodied rhetoric, then, is one strategy in a range of embodied discursive strategies through which black women understand, locate, and theorize their bodies in order to disrupt gender-exclusive definitions of race and racially exclusive definitions of gender" (40–41).

With Cooper's analysis of Anna Julia Cooper's intentional focus on Black women's entry into the public and political conversation in America alongside the first Black woman serving as first lady, we encounter a different way to read Black women's bodies, hear them speak and/or come to voice, and also interrogate the ways in which they move through this process. At times, these Black women's bodies are confined by the rules of decorum and function brilliantly within it, perfectly procuring counterlanguage to do so. This approach was used by Carol Moseley Braun during her presidential announcement speech and will be discussed in the chapter dedicated to her rhetoric. A key word to frame this communicated by Moseley Braun was "practical." This is not to say that Chisholm was not but to consider her clearly prophetic lens in charging forth in her campaign, and her lack of tolerance for anything else. Quite frankly, it could be argued she had no other choice because a lane had not been crafted nor had a route to do so been charted before her historic run. Beyond this, I will eventually contend that Kamala Harris works to combine both lenses in hopes of being practical for the political place she chooses, moment in history she is running, and hope to ride along the prophetic past she can stand upon when she is not the *first* Black woman to run for the American presidency.

Womanist rhetorical theory takes seriously the meanings, methods, and musings of Black women rhetors and the relationships they maintain as necessary to their cosmological, spiritual, social, communal, psychological, and intellectual survival and thriving. More than this, womanist rhetorical theory includes an ethic that calls forth a need to assess communication study regarding Black women rhetors through a liberative lens; thus, it is an intervention. It intervenes on behalf of Black women and is typically and most effectively used by Black women practitioners who celebrate, as opposed to demonizing, the intrinsic worth, value, and everyday experiences of Black women.

This is not to say that only Black women can generate a rhetorical analysis stemming from this theoretical frame but that Black women's experiences converge upon the tripartite oppressions that envelop the cultural, linguistic, bodily, and epistemological wisdom of being both Black and a woman in a racist, classist, sexist society. Therefore, individuals who have not consistently persistently lived in the harsh realities of Black femininity by forced biological and socially inscribed determinism may struggle to correctly read artifacts, as their bodies and voices have not been read in same, or similar, ways. While one does not necessarily have to be a womanist or claim a womanist standpoint to recognize womanist work, it is imperative to take note of the theoretical implications as they are taking place. However, to name and claim the self as womanist *is* preempted from the socially described and determined wisdom of Black femininity stemming from the violence immediately read upon certain bodies from the time the doctor claimed, as partially expressed by Shirley Chisholm, "Congratulations. It's a [Black] girl." As she is oft quoted, this is when "the emotional, sexual, and psychological stereotyping of females begins" (Vaidyanathan 2016, para 17).

This means Black women, for better or worse, have a particular understanding of the sacredness and delicate nature of what it means to be a womanist and the breadth of womanist rhetorical theory. Whether this means extrapolating arguments, providing general commentary, or even fully conceptualizing its motives, limitations, aspirations, assumptions, and even its teleological modes of operation, Black women produce womanist rhetoric, and Black women theorize about it best. For this reason, the habitation of womanist rhetoric is concealed and shrouded in the eaves of what I deem to be a trichotomous philosophical space. Traditionally, the "theoretically dense" language of critical communication scholarship is not typically attributed to rhetorical analysis focusing on the discourse of Black women. Or, put in a way to encompass the authentic contemplations of many who ascribe to the musings of heteropatriarchal white linguistic expectations of women and persons of color, only white men do critical theory in any field.

Womanist rhetorical theory is not merely a contemporary definition adopting an Afrocentric cosmological frame and adding the sentiments of a feminist methodological gaze toward rhetorical artifacts. This would be an oversimplified definition. It is a framework that adds a more rich and thorough value to Black women's speech acts otherwise missed by typical, normative ways of doing analysis. In particular, using an established frame or one typically considered established and recognizable perpetuates the cycle of diminishing

Black women's experiences in public and private life. Telling their quests from frames not charted, corralled, and tightened by their musings re-creates dismal outcomes and fashions chains that lay waste to their worldview. It also diminishes any chance for them to participate in civic life supposedly available to all citizens. Moreover, womanist rhetorical theory goes beyond the invitational rhetoric espoused by feminist communication scholars Foss and Griffin ([1995] but allows a space to exercise agency within a traditionally and historically oppressed, repressed, dispossessed, and depressed Black female body while simultaneously reconstructing a place on the shelf of the communication canon). Thus, womanist rhetorical theory allows for that "somethin that waz missin" to be called upon, "held warmly," and considered real, relevant concrete, and credible. Floyd-Thomas allots space for a fifth tenet of womanism in her text *Deeper Shades of Purple* (2006) as appropriation and reciprocity. This tenet is necessary for the second, third, and millennial waves of womanist theory, simply because intersectional research is needed to further the cause of liberation. This is where advocacy begins outside the community.

Molefi Asante noted in *Afrocentric Idea Revised* (1998) that while the goal of Afrocentricity can be seemingly essentialist, any like effort does not mute or impose death-dealing consequence upon white society in the same way. Simply put, focusing on the aspects of an African diasporic ideal, and forfeiting any other influence upon such perspectives, offers a space for liberation amid a history that has annihilated its pillars. This again recalls Floyd-Thomas's earlier noted call to ethicists and how marginalized theorists expand scholarship but do not have the cultural capital to be credited with their smart insight and critical social commentary. Altogether, womanist rhetorical theory is a call or summons for the centering of Black women's voices, experiences, and bodies (without apology) in communication scholarship. The goal of this rhetorical theory is broadly essentialist but never appropriates, discredits, undervalues, nor diminutively oversimplifies and ignores the intrinsic value of all oppressed persons and their stories of existence, resistance, and persistence against the fantastic hegemonic imagination in the field of communication and beyond. Due to its focus on the particular in an effort to empower as opposed to obtain power for the sake of power, the imperative of a womanist lens lends no further ill will toward the marginalized or others. It is a theoretical framework that demands that their discursive decisions are to be taken seriously, as they function as decisive critiques to all-white, vitriolic cannons of rhetoric. But they do not stop there. Womanist rhetorical theory—while conceived out of necessity to proclaim the human condition of terror and triumph, loss and liberation, fantastic fiction and fetishized fact as it relates to Black women's real-lived realities and how they determine they should or should not communicate them—also offers an example to the violence of hegemony. Authority can be asserted without appropriation, repression, depression, and oppression.

As communication scholars, we must appreciate Black women's ability to theorize and consider voices scattered across countless social situations and conditions amid the influence and confluence of evil exigencies working against them. Far too often, it is the epistemological privilege of marginalized persons espousing a grassroots ethic who most effectively theorize about the symbols created by the complex nature of our language and culture and how it produces certain realities. Yet they are perilously silenced and nullified as they come to voice.

Womanist rhetorical theory, consequently, stands as a useful space to chart Black women's reclaiming of voice and embodiment in positively re-created communicative spaces across disciplines, discourses, and dimensions. It also analyzes how and with what new or reconstructed tools Black women choose and use to redefine death-dealing destitution around them from the minutiae of everyday experiences to wider-reaching public speech acts. In this sense, womanist rhetorical theory considers the way Black women's words fight against white domination and patriarchal force by incorporating an ethic calling for the intrinsic worth of her own body and experiences, with a broader understanding that her privileged position facilitates a more comprehensive experience of liberation for all people on the margins.

METHODOLOGY: WOMANIST RHETORICAL CRITICISM

To frame this project, I will utilize my proposed construction of womanist rhetorical criticism built upon the works of three particular Black women: Alice Walker, Stacey Floyd-Thomas, and Kimberly P. Johnson. Floyd-Thomas's work in womanist social ethics, and Johnson's studies in womanist communication build from the literary work of Walker in ways that are pivotal to how readers, thinkers, activists, and students should approach womanist rhetoric.

Although many locate the term "womanist" within the confines of theory and definitions conflating the field with Black feminist scholarship, I argue womanism and Black feminism, while having similar social and cultural benefits for Black women, are still theoretically and ideologically different from each other. Simply explained, womanist scholars do not only intend to dismantle the house of the master but seek to build one on a different plot, using tools and a name all their own. It begins from the ground up and is rooted in the cultural wisdom and everyday struggle of the Church mothers, big mamas, and aunties of the community. Though these same women may not claim the name, the sentiments, experiences, and voice are relevant and central to the way they live their daily lives and express their truth—not as women but specifically as Black women who are the center of their families.

It is through Alice Walker that we gain the term "womanist" from her short story "Coming Apart" (1979). Although womanist scholarship in the field of communication is still growing, the history of womanism is over forty years old, dating from the release of Walker's *In Search of Our Mother's Gardens* (1983), where Walker offers a definition. She defines womanism as:

WOMANIST

1. From *womanish*. (Opp. of "girlish," i.e. frivolous, irresponsible, not serious.) A black feminist or feminist of color. From the black folk expression of mothers to female children, "you acting womanish," i.e., like a woman. Usually referring to outrageous, audacious, courageous or *willful* behavior. Wanting to know more and in greater depth than is considered "good" for one. Interested in grown up doings. Acting grown up. Being grown up. Interchangeable with another black folk expression: "You trying to be grown." Responsible. In charge. *Serious*.
2. *Also:* A woman who loves other women, sexually and/or nonsexually. Appreciates and prefers women's culture, women's emotional flexibility (values tears as natural counterbalance of laughter), and women's strength. Sometimes loves individual men, sexually and/or nonsexually. Committed to survival and wholeness of entire people, male *and* female. Not a separatist, except periodically, for health. Traditionally a universalist, as in: "Mama, why are we brown, pink, and yellow, and our cousins are white, beige and black?" Ans. "Well, you know the colored race is just like a flower garden, with every color flower represented." Traditionally capable, as in: "Mama, I'm walking to Canada and I'm taking you and a bunch of other slaves with me." Reply: "It wouldn't be the first time."
3. Loves music. Loves dance. Loves the moon. *Loves* the Spirit. Loves love and food and roundness. Loves struggle. *Loves* the Folk. Loves herself. *Regardless*.
4. Womanist is to feminist as purple is to lavender. (189)

Several scholars have utilized Walker's definition of womanism, along with the beauty, complexity, originality, truth, and grace of her writing to contextualize the experiences of Black women's lives within and outside of the African diaspora. While this text and definition provided a new rhetorical trajectory to define the specialized cognitive dissonance many Black women have felt within the feminist movement, the term "womanist" has been differently defined from its inception in social theory and critical race/gender studies.

Some scholars argue womanism is a universal term available to all women of color, or any woman sharing in the quest to eradicate the tripartite oppression of racism, sexism, and classism upon said women of color. That is not the stance taken in this argument. First, Alice Walker decisively defines a womanist as a Black woman. For the cause of communication studies, this can be taken to mean a womanist is a woman of African or African diasporic descent. Because rhetoric is built on speech acts offered by individual citizens among an audience, and "the available means of persuasion" used to craft a text, rhetoric from a womanist theoretical perspective must be centered on the voices of Black/Africana women.

Second, stemming from the idea that "naming" the self is a liberative, political, and inherently rhetorical act, womanism gives Black women the space to incorporate their feelings of difference when one term, that is "feminism," was not adopted as universal, loving the folk, and responsible. Instead, feminism became dismissive to the triple realities of race-, gender-, and class-leading Black women, particularly literary and religious scholars, to separate "for health reasons" and claim a rhetorical space of their own; however, this did not mean it was outside of the sphere of the Black community and Black men.

Clenora Hudson-Weems's *Africana Womanist Literary Theory* (2004) supports this argument by explaining that white feminism is inherently tied to Eurocentric politics, policies, productions, and tactics of persuasion. Thus, in a sense, much like Audre Lorde, though identified as a Black feminist, she considers tearing down the master's house with the master's tools an impossible task (Lorde 2002, 99). Therefore, positionality and the power to persuade are inherently tied in the importance of language and naming. Though the first wave of womanism was led squarely by composition and literary scholars, many religious scholars were leery of being overly inclusive, as the name comes from the vernacular space of Black women's experience and community. In contrast to white feminists often asserting the generalizability of all women's experiences of misogyny and sexism in American society, actual use of the term has been deemed unacceptable in some disciplines, as articulated by Hudson-Weems. However, the methodology and terminology has been helpful in shaping sociological and historiographic channels of inquiry. Many Black women authors in sociology, psychology, education, history, and medicine have not consistently utilized the term "womanist," especially before 2000, but now the social theory informs their studies as well. Hence, a project using a womanist methodology and framework are more necessary than ever to focus on the variability of Black women's activity, thought, spirituality, and responses to their respective communities to uplift and support efforts toward liberation and justice.

In spite of this, there are ways Black women reclaim their voices to speak for themselves and reimagine worlds where their bodies move beyond stagnated, liminal tropes (Cartier 2014). I contend they are able to do this, to a certain degree, within certain rhetorical spaces of their own construction by hailing a specifically charged audience. This becomes an effectively produced affective public based on principles grounded in a womanist rhetorical trajectory. Thus, my study will consider the construction, rhetoric, and heuristic value of the presidential campaign announcement speeches of Chisholm, Moseley Braun, and Harris. In order to do this, I will analyze their speeches through the lens of womanist rhetorical theory using womanist rhetorical criticism as a methodological frame. By highlighting the ways in which Black women's voices and bodies are confined and constrained by hegemonic social structures, rhetorical scholarship is better able to distinguish between structures of institutional oppression in our language in day-to-day discourse, as well as in the highest levels of government.

According to womanist rhetorician Kimberly Johnson, a womanist methodological tool of rhetorical theory would seek to find ways in which Black women come to voice amid the social, political, educational, religious, economic, and linguistic barriers attacking their progress as political agents of change and citizen-leaders. Thus, womanist rhetorical criticism is formed by asking the following questions: (1) How does the central rhetor reclaim her voice using the tenet of radical subjectivity as a liberative ethic? (2) How does the central rhetor reconstruct discursive space using the tenet of critical engagement to transform conventional communicative definitions? (3) How does the central rhetor reconstitute and reframe her epistemological privilege by accepting the tenet of redemptive self-love? (4) How does the central rhetor reimagine her audience by reforming and renorming a specific polis through traditionally communal cues, codes, and morals? As Johnson (2015) states, womanist criticism must analyze the ideology of domination that marginalizes individuals until it is able to construct a rhetorical agency that affirms the humanity of those who are marginalized. Womanism transcends our shared religious beliefs to fight for the survival and wholeness of all people because its moral arc always falls within the circumference of liberation and social justice.

In the same breath, the ideological frame of reference best articulated by Audre Lorde is conceptualized in the very fabric of womanism as she said, "For the master's tools will never dismantle the master's house. They may allow us to temporarily beat him at his own game but they will never enable us to bring about genuine change" (2002, 99). As such, critically considering the communicative trajectory of Black women's rhetoric in their presidential announcement speeches is a necessary endeavor within the study of rhetoric from a womanist perspective. Thus, womanist rhetorical criticism looks for what I call rhetorical reaction or those places within a Black woman's speech (preaching, political, or otherwise) that reclaim voice, reconstruct discursive space, reconstitute and reframe love for the self, and finally reimagine utopian possibilities to reform and renorm a more "beloved community." Typically, when Black women react in response to whiteness, they are greeted with losing employment or a severe injunction on wages, as seen in *The Help* through the characters played by Octavia Spencer and Viola Davis, or death, either physical or social. The latter is reproduced for our entertainment and enjoyment through Mrs. Sophia in *The Color Purple*. On the other hand, when they react or work to fix the fundamental destitution, despondency, and despair of their social location for the good of themselves and those they love, they can see themselves as president of the United States. They can dare to be themselves and *live*.

RHETORICAL MOVEMENTS IN WOMANIST RHETORICAL CRITICISM: A STYLE GUIDE FOR WOMANIST SPEECHES

In the field of religion, studying and using the womanist tenets as an inherent ethical compass, theological imperative, and prophetic preaching praxis of how to approach Black women's discourse offers several helpful guidelines for understanding womanist rhetoric's epistemic and prophetic side. Typically, womanist words and work can be easily applied to a realm of divine-human encounter by thinking critically about how our communicative acts must create space for justice and thriving. Beyond this, how human beings understand and/or negotiate this spiritual conversation is also captured within the wider realm of Afrocentric cosmological thought and a philosophical understanding of communal investment in our quest to overcome. However, this does not always clearly carry over into communication studies, especially for those who do not actively engage sacred rhetoric. Furthermore, rhetoric takes seriously the active voice of humans in the public square with an effort to discursively build political realities within and outside of specific communities. Therefore, it is helpful to further frame my four womanist reactions (remembering, reconstructing, reimagining, and reclaiming) alongside Johnson's (2015) call for womanist rhetorical criticism. In order to do this, I will call the elements of a speech guided by womanist rhetorical criticism as rhetorical movements. These movements adequately assess the point when the womanist rhetor admits "I was missin somethin" and considers her options of reaction. Foregrounding the theoretical rubrics of Coleman and Lorde, she has blueprints and bricks at the side of her hip.

While canonically convenient, womanist rhetorical criticism may be loosely compared to the ideological criticism of McGhee (1980) but it is not congruent. Lisa Flores (2016) makes this distinction clear by calling for communication scholars dedicated to rhetorics of race to provide theories, concepts, and ideas that function in a more robust and distinct manner. Outside of the usual tokenization of racialized perspectives and othered depictions, her article "Between abundance and marginalization: the imperative of racial rhetorical criticism" follows this consideration. Flores (2016, 4) writes,

"I suggest that the art of rhetorical criticism is concerned with politics and publics, with cultural discourses and social meanings, with rhetors and audiences. Not merely observers, rhetorical critics are social actors, guided by our theoretical knowledge, our methodological skills, and our critical senses, who seek through our work to bring both insight and judgment."

With this in mind, the typical way of *doing* the work of communication scholarship on race cannot follow traditional ideological criticism. Although communication scholar Carrie Crenshaw (1997) argues, "There is nothing essential, natural, or biological about whiteness" (255). The ways in which political communication benefits white society and male bodies Black women's voices cannot be measured by the same means. If ideological criticism and other analytical lenses wish to provide space for the marginalized voice to be heard and seen, it can neither continue to function so narrowly by missing race as a necessary element of disclosure nor fail short to challenge whiteness in its entirety. This includes its relationship to power and political structures that reinforce gendered, racialized, and classed stereotypes. Crenshaw (1997) continues to explain that "ideological rhetorical criticism reveals the vested interests protected by a particular framework for understanding social order," but it does not consistently highlight the value of race and positionality and vested interest.

In the same way marginalized scholars squarely name their audience, alliance, and membership in specific groups, by Crenshaw's definition the function of ideological rhetorical criticism must follow. Yet womanist theory distinguishes itself through uplifting race as a category of epistemic privilege, thereby reclaiming agency and affirmation. That which is experienced as an unremarkable burden is refashioned as an incomparable ideological blessing with otherworldly possibilities. In this way, the womanist rhetor embodies the conceptualization of *Maat*, which "became identified with truth, righteousness, justice, order, balance, harmony and reciprocity" (Asante 2001, 49). Asante, also summarizing Karenga's (2004) ideas, brought him to the conclusion that not only is *Maat* central to an Afrocentric vision of communication, but it is comparable to values of virtue in other cultural conceptions. Essentially, for womanist rhetorical criticism and a womanist rhetorical theory, the movements are centered in the way in which Black women craft their own solutions, outside of and within white heteropatriarchal structures that lack reciprocity, harmony, balance, order, justice, righteousness, and truth in effort to redefine discourse that is wholesome, is fair, and gives voice to the voiceless.

Consequently, the rhetorical movements include navigating the choices of the everyday through space, place, audience, and commitment to specific political platforms. Where these Black women decide to speak; who these Black women choose to speak to, about, on behalf of or for; and whom they invite into their audience are imperative considerations when analyzing a text from a womanist perspective. Ultimately, their communicative commitments or political platforms either radically reject whiteness, as a whole, or they focus on ways to safely peel away at the productions of white patriarchy through economic and political capital. Thus, the rhetorical movements are as follows: (1) textual reflection—the movement that captures the rhetorical task at hand, what is actually being said within the space, also known as "the message behind the message"; (2) physical setting—the movement that calls the space into being/where the speech is delivered and for whom it is actually created; (3) the womanist audience—the movement in which the affective public forms from those who are invited to hear and participate as full partners toward thriving (allies are not to be assumed); and (4) coming to voice—the movement measuring the moment the rhetor's audience can hear her personal reaffirmation and reclamation of the *imago dei*. Functioning through these movements in public space, Black women incorporating this vision invite other Black women to stand in solidarity to do the same. To some degree, the speeches can be characterized as "womanist" or "womanish," but more importantly, methodically traversing through each movement equips us with another tool to evaluate womanist words, ways, wit, and wisdom.

"CHOSEN AS A PIONEER": CHARLOTTA AMANDA SPEARS BASS AND WOMANIST POLITICAL SPEECH CONTEXTUALIZATION OF BASS

Toward the tail end of World War II and advancing toward the political stage in the era of McCarthyism and the Red Scare, Charlotta Amanda Spears Bass was already stepping forward as a political activist in the Black community of Los Angeles. Bass was in a class all her own. Purposely situating herself as a "Negro woman" and accepting the responsibility as a "chosen pioneer," Bass was committed to the plight of the underserved and underprivileged. During her 1952 vice-presidential campaign for the Progressive Party some twenty years before Chisholm's historic run for president, she became a visionary to lead the way in defining Black women's political voice. Owner and operator of the *California Eagle*, Bass did not originally strive to go into the world of presidential politics. Yet her activism at the forefront of Black women and men's rights in the state of California made her popular with the masses, as well as leaving her open to critical surveillance from the federal government. While there are some studies committed to this remarkable rhetor and activist, her acceptance speech remains available for analysis. I argue it is one of the earliest, if not the only, available rubric to closely consider womanist rhetoric among political communicators and presidential candidates in this country engaging a call to civic service. As such, I name her a protowomanist: a Black woman centering her voice and vision around her personal experiences in an era denying her the chance to come into her full potential.

Movement 1: Textual Reflection or the Spoken Word

Bass's words and actions continue to cut through and into the viscous nature of a racist, sexist, classist, and altogether malevolent reality she and other Black women of her time and today have to endure. Such vision and virtue allowed space for Black women to follow in her footsteps and to further set the stage for civic disruption on the grounds of equality, equity, inclusion, and advancement. This was her promise to the Progressive Party and her larger audience of Americans suffering on the margins. Although scholars did not incorporate the word "womanist" or "womanish" in their work until well after the Black Power movement, a *womanish* spirit has been well exhibited and understood among most Black lay audiences (Alston 2006). Bass's speech carries this spirit.

She begins by saying, "I stand before you with great pride," unapologetically full of herself. Not to be misread as cockiness, Bass immediately recognizes that her feet are planted in a historical moment. It indeed, is a historical feat, to be the first Black woman to stand as a running mate for the highest office in the land. This unyielding confidence adds a captivating and crucial authority to her words. More than this, she notes that while "it is a great honor to be chosen as a pioneer," she also acknowledges it is also "a great responsibility" (Kelly 2020). Knowing herself and what she is capable of achieving, Bass foregrounds a strident sense of radical subjectivity and dares to stand firm in her right/rite to stake claim as a political aspirant.

Movement 2: Physical and Psychological Setting

On Sunday, March 30, 1952, Bass gave her acceptance speech for the vice-presidential nomination to represent the Progressive Party. The convention, held in Chicago, was a pivotal moment in her career but also modeled the ways many Black women in politics are steadfastly rooted in the conditions and realities of those who look like them and share similar experiences. Although her speech was not given in a historically Black space, such as a historically Black college or university or a Black Church with a majority Black membership or denominational affiliation, the physical and psychological setting of the Progressive Party afforded her the opportunity to speak freely, liberally, and with a heart toward justice and equality. At that time, well-known Black actor, athlete, and activist Paul Robeson was the national cochairperson of the group. Vincent Hallihan, a lawyer known for his dedication to labor reform, was the presidential candidate for the party and Bass's running mate.

Following the election of 1952, the Progressive Party, one of the most open, affirming, and liberal parties of its time, dismantled. The dissolution could certainly be connected to a platform that informed welcome ideals of American communists. Former vice-president and leader of the party Henry Wallace purposely picked Bass to broaden the political ambitions of the party after witnessing her potential. Likewise, Chicago is one of the primary thoroughfares of Black migration from the South and had several Black women and men to build an audience, in comparison to places such as Sumter, South Carolina, the birthplace of Bass or even Los Angeles, her newfound home. During the time of the speech, exact demographics of the audience are not available, yet, whether open or absent in physical presence, Bass calls upon the giants upon whose shoulders she stands. She states: "I am strengthened by thousands on thousands of pioneers who stand by my side and look over my shoulder—those who have led the fight for freedom—those who led the fight for women's rights—those who have been in the front line fighting for peace and justice and equality everywhere. How they must rejoice in this great understanding, which here joins the cause of peace and freedom. These pioneers, the living and the dead, men and women, black and white, give me strength and a new sense of dedication" (1952). Interestingly, Bass calls upon her audience, whether able to physically hear her voice, or witnessing in the spirit realm, a womanist commitment to traditional communalism, or "the folk'" is understandably present in this speech.

Movement 3: Womanist Audience

To further define her audience, Bass demonstrates she is neither afraid nor ashamed to tell her audience precisely who she is: a "Negro woman." While her opening comments appeal to her femininity as a global experience of what it may mean to become the party's representative, she is clear that she is not Whitney Houston's *Every Woman*, nor does she simply reach further into the future and extend a call in saying, "[OK] ladies[, now] let's get in formation" as Beyoncé does. Embedded in the space of her speech is a womanist audience that understands what it means to be a Black woman, knowing that the next fight on the news could be filmed and noted from your very doorstep. Although her forty years at the *California Eagle* had been painted with success, she understood the surveillance and racist backlash she was receiving affected her health and shut down its printer. As she decided to focus on political pursuits, we see that her words are clear with the rationale of her new role, solely as an activist and political pioneer. She states, "I could not retire and step aside when Rose Lee Ingram and her two boys were railroaded to jail for defending themselves. Could I turn a deaf ear to Rosalie McGee? Where was that Shangri-La in these United States where I could live and breathe in dignity? Where my people enjoyed the rights for which their sons and nephews died? In the North there were the Trenton Six demanding justice; in the Middle West was Cicero. In the South there stood Amy Mallard, the Martinsville Seven, and unnamed hundreds of unavenged deaths that cried out. There was no rest in Florida—there a cross was burning and a bomb killed Harriet Moore and her husband; and white justice sniffed out the life of Samuel Shepherd, threatened Lee Irvin" (Bass 1952). Calling the roll of women and men who died at the hands of white supremacist violence and racist injustice, she is clear that her fight is for those who identify with this experience. While there is a place for womanist allies, the epistemological privilege of those who share in the same or similar experiences (and opportunities to experience oppression) outweigh any global feminist goal.

Movement 4: Coming to Voice

Speaking truth to power, crafting a specific audience, and painting a vision of clear commitments is imperative to observe in the rhetorical movements of womanist speech. Yet incorporating the tenet of redemptive self-love—or what I consider the principle of radically redeeming and reimagining a possible future for the self and acknowledgment that we, as Black women, are made in the image of God—is paramount to womanist speech. Always and already women who are rhetorically and politically afforded the protections of whiteness enjoy their femininity as heiresses with the same priceless dowry tag life has to offer, and even Mastercard may not be able to cover. This is not the case for Black women. Bruised and broken in by the systemic and institutionalized scoffing of white society, some of us are simply brave. Bass attests to this by explaining, "I stand. . . ." (1952).

In the first two words of her acceptance speech, before she admits "great pride" she has in being before her audience, she "stands." To love oneself, particularly, as a Black woman is as simple as standing. Possibly anxious and a bit afraid of the ensuing challenges to come, Bass is not ashamed. She does not hide behind an invitational rhetoric to hear out the conversation points of anyone in a parking lot, nor does she have time for frivolous rhetoric. Standing in front of a presumably majority white audience, though handpicked for her promise, poise, and potential, Bass truly lives into the title of Hull, Bell-Scott, and Smith's influential text *All the Women Are White, All the Blacks Are Men, but Some of Us Are Brave*. Simply standing there, alone and maybe afraid, directly next to the embodied presence of whiteness and surrounded by possible naysayers, she begins standing and ends with the command "Let My People Go," calling back to the prophet Moses, who was a spokesperson for the God of Israel. This strategy to rhetorically align herself with a historical prophetic figure is not only associated with the African American prophetic tradition but also demonstrates an affinity to protowomanist leanings toward traditional communalism and the importance of divine symbolism.

Quickly overviewing the speech of Bass allows us to set parameters for understanding womanism and womanist rhetorical theory as its intellectual musings will be used as a foundational base for understanding and analyzing the announcement speeches of Chisholm, Moseley Braun, and Harris. Furthermore, it extends a historically relevant line of demarcation for Black women's voices in the political sphere over and against white women's intellectual sensibilities, social responsibilities, and political commitments. Bass's involvement on the front lines of Black liberation and communal uplift not only presented her before the community as a "chosen pioneer," but more importantly as a choice candidate for a new beginning. Her rhetoric and sensibilities are protowomanist because her goals point toward the striving of an entire people. The sort of wisdom and inherent prowess Bass demonstrated, builds from the usual wisdom that is represented in the everyday Black woman, no matter her social surroundings.

Womanist wisdom exists in the sacredness of the everyday existential quandaries, ontological struggles, and phenomenological truths of everyday Black women. It exists in a plane of prophetic witnessing I would deem as epistemic rhetoric that celebrates the body and highlights vocalized experience over and against that which is grounded in the metaphysical musings of the masses that trample on the marginalized. Throughout history, its mantel has been taken up by Black woman rhetors, who serve not simply as spokespersons but itinerant intercessors serving in between the pulpit and the pew; beyond the podium and the prayer circle; and through the crafting of the pen in rarely read poetry and song. It is created from hands weaving together communal memories. It quilts a comforting and divine love for all wanting to purely experience its alacrity, warmth, honesty, and hospitality. More than this, it is tasted in the well-seasoned food that praises the souls who are cast onto the margins of a society that silences and stifles them, and it is never wasted.

A womanist style of speech, as demonstrated through the analysis of Bass's vice-presidential acceptance speech, does not accept the myth that says Black women have no intellectual dearth, nor do they have theory. They remain faithful to the mark of a high calling that is not simply eschatological in nature. As Bass declares, womanist speech says: "I will not retire nor will I retreat, not one inch, so long as God gives me vision to see what is happening and strength to fight for the things I know are right. For I know that my kingdom, my peoples of all the world, is not beyond the skies, the moon and the stars but right here at our feet—acres of diamonds—freedom—peace and justice—for all the peoples if we will but stoop down and get them" (1952). Womanist speech is not thrown away for the dogs to devour, nor does it accept the outcast, downtrodden position society tries to arrange for it to remain. It is full. It is confident. It tastes of liberation, empowerment, fairness, justice, equity, and inclusion—for a whole people. For it *is* far better than Campbell's soup.

CONCLUSION

Throughout this manuscript, I count the presidential campaign announcement speeches of Chisholm, Moseley Braun, and Harris, not as sacred text but as sacred moments and movements in which Black women navigate through ways and means toward political success. Their communicative acts are curated from the ways their identities as Black women drastically inform their ideas. In my preliminary summation, only Chisholm and Moseley Braun provided speeches following the more stringent rubric of womanist rhetorical theory. Harris seemed to be constructing something altogether different, leaving questions for what kind of speech making is successful among a wider audience in common time or outside a presidential cycle riddled with pandemic panic and frenzied fallout. However, by sifting through the ways they use traditional rhetorical devices, and then do their own redemptive rhetorical work, I find that the themes and theories they create along the way are much richer for establishing womanist rhetorical criticism, than simply doing a line-by-line analysis of their words. This work can be done later. For now, I contend the most important task should be critically assessing their intellectual adroitness and methodological malleability inside the pulpits, behind podiums and upon the platforms which they dare to be themselves. In conclusion, womanist rhetorical criticism through the arm of womanist rhetorical theory allows us to see the virtue in the Black woman's voice, embodied discourse, and, more importantly, her ability to chart out her theoretical imperative for herself, those she loves, and those who are also living on the margins of society.

Chapter 3

"I Ran Because Somebody Had to Do It First"

The Presidential Campaign Announcement Speech of Congresswoman Shirley Chisholm

> I ran for the presidency, despite hopeless odds, to demonstrate the sheer will and refusal to accept the status quo.
> —SHIRLEY CHISHOLM

INTRODUCTION

At the core of Chisholm's statement captioning this chapter, her words rationalize the wisdom, knowledge, and fortitude many Black women forged during the civil rights movement. Heralding such a strong conscious toward being "responsible" is not only *womanish* (Alston) but wily (Coleman) and central to womanist thought as outlined by Walker's (1983) definition and expounded upon through Floyd-Thomas's (2006) tenets. Chisholm was not running *just because* but for a cause, thus exuding and exemplifying the collective energy of womanist commitment. This commitment toward seeking a path to build and buttress the opportunity for others demonstrates more than a feminist ideology typically targeted at deconstructing patriarchy and class stratification. It details the focus toward the "survival of a whole people, male and female" (Walker 1983). Such was also the motto of the National Association of Colored Women "lifting as we climb," encapsulated in this womanist leadership style is a dedication and deep appreciation for the collective strivings of "Black folk." Chisholm not only broke down barriers and cracked glass ceilings but proved to be more formidable than any of her opponents imagined possible.

According to Asante (2007), "Those who followed [Chisholm] believed that a person should be able to run for the presidency regardless of race or gender. They also accepted the fact that there were so many whites that believed in the inferiority of Blacks that it would be hard for a Black person to be elected to the presidency" (108). Her campaign to become a representative for her Bedford-Stuyvesant community was built on her early career in education and civic engagement in democratic clubs, fundraising, and organization. In her text *Unbought and Unbossed*, Chisholm also notes that living between Barbados and New York around a tightknit family consistently entertaining community members who were civically engaged for the economic empowerment and improvement of Black people piqued her early interest in politics.

Lifting the values of her community and setting her sights on the common people and their "potential" may not have yielded her enough delegates to move beyond the Democratic primary, but it did crack glass in 1972. This was made possible through a presidential announcement speech that harkened upon the best of the Black rhetorical tradition. Central to the style of African American rhetoric is an audience that is built by call-and-response and the general sense of collectivism. Building not simply from the harshness of enslavement and race-based segregation, the influence of *Maat*, which includes balance, order, audience, and spirituality, is paramount to building an effective argument and audience that will take up the charge to act. Outside of the typical focus on Eurocentric persuasive techniques, Chisholm's speech set the gold standard for the Black women and men who ran after her, particularly when considering womanist approaches toward rhetorical theory and engaging speech writing and performance.

Theorizing through Watkins-Dickerson and Johnson (2019), I contend that Chisholm's announcement speech serves as a model of a womanist style, building a blueprint for the African American political audience. This, then, makes way for a decidedly womanist approach due to a strong dedication to the womanist tenet of traditional communalism. Her speech and rhetorical persona demonstrate why a specifically womanist ideological categorization matters in rhetorical theory and how it can affect political communication and promotes agentive space for the constituents joining the audience. Utilizing womanist rhetorical criticism and outlining her presidential announcement speech given at Concord Baptist Church, I will consider the ways in which the womanist tenets are presented. This will allow me to determine if she follows the four movements typical of a womanist rhetorical structure considering the spoken word, the physical and psychological setting of the speech, whether or not she establishes a womanist audience, and whether or not she "comes to voice."

CONTEXTUALIZATION OF CHISHOLM

Born November 30, 1924, in New York to Barbadian parents, Shirley Anita St. Hill Chisholm was born in the same year that President Calvin Coolidge was sworn into the office of president of the United States. In his text *The Power of the American Presidency 1789–2000* political science scholar Michael A. Genovese (2001) cited George Creel's description of Coolidge as being "distinguishable from the furniture only when he moved" (126). Despite his efforts to "Keep it cool with Coolidge," what could be considered as such a nonchalant attitude in his vision for the office "built up a meager record" (128). Genovese notes, "He shrunk the presidency and left several key problems unaddressed. His failure to supply leadership, to recognize and even anticipate problems, contributed to the Great Depression" (128). This era leading up to the Great Depression left many immigrant families like Chisholm's in a precarious position. While her parents worked to save money for their children's education and future, Chisholm and her siblings were sent back to Barbados. Consequently, her childhood was formed by two competing ideals: American exceptionalism and fast-paced city life versus the comfort of country living, strong family bonds, and communal uplift.

In a land often celebrated with glowing opportunities for those upholding the American mythos of a "city upon a hill" or the "land of opportunity," immigrants in the 1920s experienced a great deal of hardship and difficulty. While Upton Sinclair's (1906) well-celebrated turn of the century novel *The Jungle* demonstrated the desolate working and living conditions for immigrant families looking for a better life in the United States, Pauline Hopkins's *Contending Forces* ([1900] 1988) came a few years before, marking the social, economic, and political difficulties of Blackness and womanhood in America. What we learn from authors like Hopkins in regard to the framing of Chisholm as a womanist rhetor, the use of fictional accounts to paint a picture for the white literary imagination provides a structural understanding of how racism and anti-Black sexism function in a classist society. Jennifer Putzi (2004) argues that Hopkins's distinct focus on the stigma of embodied Blackness combined with being a woman created a specific set of challenges for them.

For example, in "'Raising the Stigma': Black Womanhood and the Marked Body in Pauline Hopkins's 'Contending Forces'" (1988), Putzi argues, "The slave marked with scars could be seen as a victim in need of assistance but very rarely a man or woman capable of agency" (1). Acknowledging the "embodied stigma" Black women must experience is imperative to considering the way they must frame their rhetorical persona, in both public and private spaces. Throughout the novel, Hopkins deals with the ways in which various Black women (and the Black men around them) renegotiate space, words, opportunity, and spirituality in an effort to perform survival in postemancipation life. Amid different and difficult arguments, Hopkins, through literature, demonstrates the presence of raced-based sexism and the way in which the two categories impose upon economic stability and upward political movement. In the preface of her famed novel, Hopkins states, "Fiction is of great value to any people as a preserver of manners and customs—religious, political and social. It is a record of growth and development from generation to generation" (13). Hopkins and other Black woman novelists have been capable of centering the discursive realities of Black women's experience in the "land of the free" and juxtaposed it behind an uncanny and unfair political backdrop.

Patricia Watkins also demonstrates the centrality of political rhetoric in Hopkins's works in "Rape, Lynching, Law, and 'Contending Forces': Pauline Hopkins—Forerunner of Critical Race Theorists" (2003). Not only does Watkins highlight the ways in which Hopkins foregrounds real historical matters like Putzi (2004), but she also considers the legal ramifications of rape, lynching, and silence in the Black community. As it relates to Chisholm and the other women considered in this book, I assert that Watkins highlights the importance of elevating Hopkins as a foremother to critical race and gender theory. Not only should Hopkins be celebrated for this, but her work also outlines the ways in which the American political structure discursively disavows space for Black women to progress. The various testimonies of Black women working to climb up a political system built to buttress the aims of white men functions against them in several ways. One of those is by imposing silence upon Black men. The other is by imposing an ideological construct that frames the lives and liberties of Black femininity, womanhood, and motherhood into either a version of a mammy or jezebel. These caricatures (and others) have historically been cast in a manner that is opposite of society's ideal leadership material, certainly unfit for the office of the presidency. Therefore, those Black men (and women) who dare go against the grain must pay the price, one way or another.

In her pamphlet *Southern Horrors: Lynch Law and All its Phases* ([1892] 2004), Memphian journalist and historian Ida B. Wells detailed the horrific accounts of Black men's lynching and spoke out regarding the harsh policies, laws, and rhetorical fallacies placed onto the character of Black men. Her witness and activism also demonstrated the ways in which Black women have always been at the fore of civil rights rhetoric, and the uplifting of the community, much to the ideals projected by the campaign of Chisholm. Wells's sentiments not only were foregrounded in Hopkins's novel but shaped the rhetorical trajectory of Black feminist and womanist thought and speech. This rhetorical lineage was inherent throughout Chisholm's presidential campaign announcement speech, as well as her political service. Though obtaining some voting rights some eighty years apart, Black women and men were still working to subvert and steer through an unwelcoming political system.

The same "lies" not so passively highlighted in Chisholm's speech and autobiography were exposed years before through the writing and oral expositions of Wells. When considering womanist rhetorical theory and finding its historical and political roots, Wells practiced what she preached. She did not plainly theorize about the violence of her time but published extensively and delivered jarring speeches to audiences detailing the racist laws of the United States and the deafening silence imposed upon their being. In her book chapter "To Call a Thing by Its True Name: The Rhetoric of Ida B. Wells" from *Reclaiming Rhetorica: Women in the Rhetorical Tradition*, Jacquelyn Jones Royster (1995) explains: "[Wells] spent little or no time discussing abstract notions of the ways and means of rhetorical effectiveness, as philosophers of rhetoric have done, she did spend considerable time engaging in rhetorical acts and demonstrating rhetorical eloquence and expertise. Wells had her eyes on action, and she seemed much more inclined to practice rather than preach the rhetorical arts. She accomplished this task with flair and style, leaving behind a provocative image of language well used. Ida B. Wells engaged in writing as swordsmanship, demonstrating that in the right hands the pen can in-deed become a mighty sword" (169). While Wells worked to explain how lynching was inherently tied to institutionalized white patriarchy, Chisholm frames the Nixon administration as "deceitful" and "lying" and says that Americans are "intelligent." Eighty years prior to Chisholm's run for office and more than fifty years later, the violence over and against the Black body continues to perpetuate a system of control that stirs against their agentive voice. Wells and Chisholm share a similar sentiment to expose a system built on the backs of Black women (and men) and benefiting from the lies that impose harm upon them.

Through enslavement, Black women's bodies served as a both product and productive force between policy and production. This reality arguably exists today as well. Black women from Wells's or Chisholm's time may not have shaped the world or served as the face of its political economy; however, through their pain and suffering, their embodied stigma has allowed them an edge. Thus, the epistemological privilege oppressed peoples, specifically from Black women, necessitates the truth-telling and lie-shaming qualities of Wells, Hopkins, and Chisholm in order to spring forth new possibilities for a future generation of survival, thriving, and liberation. Reimagining such a world was part and parcel of the rhetoric these three women built their careers upon, and Chisholm displays this foundation within her speech and overall rhetorical persona. In particular, womanist theologian Linda Thomas argues that this sense of "reconstruction" is necessary in the process of liberation, hope, and possibilities for all those on the margins.

In her essay "Womanist Theology, Epistemology, and a New Anthropological Paradigm" (1998) womanist theologian Linda Thomas states:

> Admittedly, reconstructing knowledge is like tearing down a formidable edifice that has been built over an extensive number of years. The structure was designed by architects who had a clear vision of what the end product would be like and used only the most advanced technical devices for its erection. The architects guaranteed that the materials used would be permanent and indestructible. The building is, of course, our minds and the architects are those who historically have represented patriarchal, white European cultures. A womanist, in her reconstruction of knowledge, must not only be a diligent craft per son, she must develop an approach that utilizes the kind of technology that can dismantle the seeming indestructibility of the original building materials. (493)

Such real-life examples of this exist as recent as Hurricane Katrina (2005), as explored by Black feminist sociologist Melissa Harris-Perry in *Sister Citizen: Shame, Stereotypes, and Black Women in America* (2011) and as far back as Harriet Jacobs's *Incidents in the Life of a Slave Girl* ([1861] 2009). Therefore, when considering the classed categories of race and gender and the background shaping Chisholm's rhetorical persona, speech writing, performance, eloquence, and command of her audience, analyzing her campaign speech at the intersections of her Blackness, femininity, educational attainment, and even her immigrant identity help foreground the womanist style that is present.

For instance, according to the online source files of the African-American Migration Experience (2020), there are thirteen movements of Africans into America, with only two being coerced. Those were the transatlantic slave trade and the domestic slave trade. During the early twentieth century and before World War I, many Caribbean immigrants came to the southern region of the United States as skilled workers, especially from British colonies like Jamaica and Barbados. However, after the Great Depression, and due to political instability, more and more people from various parts of the Caribbean made the United States home. Due to this influx of immigrants, though skilled and well educated, the US Congress imposed restrictive actions to keep them from obtaining entry. Although ethnocentric, nationalist practices were used to keep Irish and Eastern European white immigrants in the slums and without equal opportunity, even more did immigration policies affect the Black population.

The African-American Migration Experience explains, "The Immigration Act of 1924 drastically turned the tide of Caribbean immigration to the United States. It plummeted from 10,630 in 1924 to only 321 in 1925.... The law stipulated an immigration quota system of 2 percent of the foreign-born for each nationality enumerated in the 1890 census" (2020, para 35). These quotas reinforced white supremacist, racist ideals and encouraged the formation of labor unions, pan-Africanism, and even the departure of some. Fighting against the systemic xenophobia of American exceptionalism should have brought together immigrants, due to their shared class difficulties; however, this was not always the case. Of course, "Northwestern Europe was favored in this system, while those from the European colonies could only enter under the designated quota allotted to their colonial masters.... The Caribbean migration was kept low, never rising in the late 1920s and 1930s to the levels reached before the 1924 legislation" (para 36). With the Depression came a decrease in immigrant interest and many returned to their homeland, based on the combined problems of financial stability in an unfavorable and unwelcoming country promoting a restrictive immigration policy. Even though immigrants, like Chisholm's parents, were working beyond the political and economic system to obtain equality and opportunity, no matter their level of education and skill, Black women and men from the Caribbean were not consistently welcome. No doubt, this could have informed Chisholm's understanding of the necessity of community, faith, education, and more.

Chisholm explained in her autobiography that her family raised her with a keen awareness that education could open opportunities. In particular, she believed that anyone focusing on their abilities to achieve could do so. However, she was still aware of the social conditions women, POC, and Black women, in particular, consistently and persistently have to work against, no matter their level of attainment. In particular, being Black and a woman offered particular challenges. Whether on the political stage or not, these ontological markers of identity can immobilize Black women's upward ability in American society. Certainly, Coolidge's lackluster presidency and the ensuing conditions he passively created can suggest a direct correlation between Chisholm's upbringing back and forth from Barbados to the United States. Though her parents' moves to find work and stability between two spaces is not the main purpose of this chapter, contextualizing Chisholm in order to understand the potential relationship between a more broadly established Black communal identity is. Yet it is no coincidence that the mediocrity and lackadaisical moods, manners, and mindsets of white heteropatriarchal leadership at our nation's fore have signaled (then and now) a need for individuals on the margins of society to refuse complacency. It elicits and illuminates the need to call for change in the communities around them. This is what Chisholm stood for in her presidential campaign, and this mantra was represented in the words of her speech. President Calvin Coolidge's presidency is a key example of how hegemonic masculine structures reproduce institutionalized discrimination and systemic failures. As such, these agreed upon American ideals only protect and proliferate causes and cases that offer privilege and protection by their race, class, and gender. Empty promises remain unquestioned and unchallenged and questioning who is qualified for the task remains an issue for those challenging the status quo.

Not only true for Coolidge, the seemingly nonchalant acquiescence to do "nothing" about the problems that face the American population consistently drives citizens into great disappointment and distrust of political leaders. Thus, Chisholm's campaign was more than a woman or a Black person running for president. Her "unbought and unbossed" mantra depicted her as an *unbothered* candidate. Unbothered did not mean that the effects of misogynoir did not affect her well-being but that because of it she still stood as a candidate that was mindful, wily, and smart enough to see the bigger picture. Some would say she kept her "eyes on the prize." Her persona is not simply a radicalized "folding chair feminism" but the core of womanist rhetoric in the makings. As Condoleezza Rice once said, "People who end up as 'first' don't actually set out to be first. They set out to do something they love." By demonstrating her dedication to being *first*, "because somebody had to do it," demonstrates Chisholm's love, commitment, and awareness of her Blackness and the particular brand of sexism and misogyny she would face on the campaign trail.

AN OVERVIEW: CHISHOLM'S SPEECH AND WOMANIST RHETORICAL STYLE

In her presidential announcement speech, Chisholm does not claim a particular theoretical, ideological, philosophical, or political standpoint. Furthermore, the scholarly and social language of the term "womanist" was not necessarily available to her. However, in many ways, womanist rhetorical theory considers not simply the "art of (her) persuasion" or the mere act of "enchanting the soul" of others. It is more complex and more comprehensive. The womanist rhetor (only) speaks based on her embodied experience. Thus, charting the workings of a womanist rhetorical style of speech lies in the overall manner the rhetor distinctively launches discursive techniques. These techniques must not only center their epistemological purview as Black women who are forged by the world around them but also welcome engagement with it historically, politically, economically, educationally, spiritually, and most importantly, communally.

Beyond being a radical, liberal, Marxist, or even a Black feminist, Chisholm reaches into the pocket of her past built on her multiple identities. She speaks into her audience a promise for the future only an administration like hers could provide. She offers the pathway toward a holistic experience the common person can bring to an office, theoretically created to speak for the people and represent everyone but historically has only kept white supremacy and patriarchy at the fore. Because the thesis of her speech is not mesmerized with the focus on class structural systems tied to patriarchy, her tone is purely womanist. In between her words and sentiments exists not an effort to distance herself from the Black community nor the women's liberation movement altogether but to clarify and solidify her commitment to her Blackness and femininity. Thus, she utilizes a womanist framework that acknowledges her different, not deficient experience in the world.

In a 1989 reprint of her 1970 essay "Racism and Anti-Feminism" for *The Black Scholar* Chisholm opens by explaining, "America has been sufficiently sensitized as to whether or not black people are willing to both fight and die for their rights to make the question itself asinine and superfluous. America is not yet sufficiently aware that such a question applied to women is equally asinine and superfluous" (2). Her efforts within the speech work to clarify this previously expressed standpoint. Now, as a politician, she is dedicated to doing the work of not only redistributing power but also pushing the country and her community. Chisholm enters into a political space that has yet to be experienced. In the next immediate paragraph of the essay, she further explains: "I am both black and a woman. That is a good vantage point from which to view at least two elements of what is becoming a social revolution: the American Black Revolution and the Women's Liberation Movement. But it is also a horrible disadvantage. It is a disadvantage because America, as a nation, is both racist and anti-feminist. Racism and anti-feminism are two of the prime traditions of this country" (Chisholm [1970] 1989, 2).

Two years after the essay is published, these same reflections are carried into her presidential announcement speech. She benefits neither from whiteness or a masculine identity. Having little to no institutionalized power, is a fact of her reality, even as an educated member of Congress. In the essay, she paints a picture to address the lack of involvement of women in politics but also skillfully displays the difficulty Black women have in working toward communal change. These words passively reverberate through her speech and call for nationwide improvement of opportunities for all standing on the margins.

In the opening of her speech, she actively signifies that she is "not the candidate for Black America, although I am Black and proud," refusing to deny the two entry points of her epistemological privilege. Her announcement speech and overall reality encounters more than just the Black experience of her political contemporaries, such as Charles Rangel, Ralph Metcalf, and the other thirteen members of the Congressional Black Caucus or the Women's Caucus. Chisholm was a founding member of both. Yet, as the sole female founding member of the Black Caucus, she encountered sexism and misogyny. By the same token, it was far different than the limitations imposed by white society, and even women like Margaret Chase Smith or fellow Democratic representative of Michigan Martha Griffiths experienced a certain level of privilege by not having to work through anti-Black racism. Due to this, her entry into general feminist discourse, was not immediately celebrated with all women positioning themselves in her camp.

Potentially considering this, she then declares, "I am not the candidate for the feminist movement in this country, although I am a woman, and equally proud of that." By highlighting her identity, a normative analysis may assume she rejects her Blackness and femininity as a realpolitik and standpoint and incorrectly push readers and hearers to categorize Chisholm as an intersectional Black feminist. However, I contend this is an oversimplification and she is doing something much more. Chisholm is instead drafting a style all her own. It is one that clearly welcomes her subject positions, without rejecting either identity but also forging a pathway for others to follow. This is not with the burden of being the *first*, instead it is with the blessing of being chosen to do so. She is both Black and a woman.

While a womanist style of speech does not mean the rhetor can only re-create rhetorical space using solely Afrocentric language and ideals. It simply means that the ideals are foregrounded physically, physiologically, psychologically, and even prophetically. This may be through incorporating traditionally white verbiage and concepts in the syntactic structure of the overall speech and using it to the speaker's strengths within the space. Based on the way in which her speech uses conventional rhetorical devices to illuminate the problems of the country at that time, she does not pander but build from a unique audience who value "the least of these." Those "regular" citizens of the United States that are suffering from the "political fat cats" and unfair policies in place. In essence, one could argue she does not play conventional politics, and instead engages in something new, different, and decidedly centered on a construct that favors those that have been forgotten, left to the side, and ignored. Overall, the womanist style displayed in the reading and hearing of Shirley Chisholm's speech is the recrafting of a Black woman's embodied voice, presence, experience, knowledge, and prowess within a speech given to the backdrop of an authentically Black place, space, and audience. These three considerations are what truly render a Black political audience. What makes the speech inherently womanist in my contention is the fact Chisholm artfully crafts, imagines, and delivers the speech in a manner that speaks to all that are present but beyond the metaphysical realities white onlookers can conceive. The womanist rhetor does it first, not only because "somebody had to do it," but because she has the will, the way, the wisdom, and the wit to speak with authority, passion, eloquence, and careful astuteness through her delivery of a liberative message for the community she loves. Cheering her on at certain moments, the once Black religious audience, peaks their attention to the inherently Gospel-centered message of Chisholm that works to "tell the truth and shame the devil," an oft-noted saying that parallels "speaking truth to power," no matter the consequence.

By using what Marcyliena Morgan (2002) calls "counterlanguage" in her text *Language, Discourse, and Power in African American Culture*, Chisholm holds the interests of Black women, like herself, at heart, while also buttressing a new definition of who "the people" of the United States are, who they can be, and what they can achieve together. During enslavement, the postemancipation South, and well into the 1960s, Morgan contends that counterlanguage carried with it a sense of doubly constructed talk or a message potentially carrying more than one interpretation. The audience was composed of a purely Black audience, but the rhetor understood spies may be in earshot and messages may be overheard. Therefore, maintaining the integrity or ethos of a trusted speaker and/or representative was paramount, while also considering the extended audience that may be listening. Morgan (2002) states, "the counterlanguage included multiple audiences, layers of understanding and concomitant multiple subjectivities. It may not have survived and been adapted were it not for dominant Southern society's relentless monitoring of African Americans' communication and language. Irrespective of the reason for its continued significance in African American interactions, the counterlanguage is the foundation of all African American discourse" (25). Using this concept, I argue that the conventional rhetorical devices in Chisholm's announcement speech remain on the surface of her message, considering the type of audience Morgan says includes "all black hearers and potential hearers, as well as the likelihood that there were spies and overhearers/reporters" (25). In the next section of this chapter, I will consider the speech itself and the response of Chisholm's audience.

COMBINING CONVENTION AND COUNTERLANGUAGE: THE USE OF RHETORICAL DEVICES IN CHISHOLM'S ANNOUNCEMENT SPEECH AS WOMANIST INGENUITY OR REDEFINITION

As articulated in the beginning of this study, womanist rhetorical theory conceptualizes the embodied discursive truths of Black femininity and the wisdom it carries and brings forth. Usually, this is missed or dismissed by conventional methods of rhetorical analysis and speech study. Womanist and Black feminist scholars inside and outside of the field of communication have written about the difficulty Black women experience as they "come to voice," but few have detailed methods to show how they do it inside and outside of white audiences. Charting several of the rhetorical devices used in Chisholm's presidential campaign speech after contextualizing her rhetorical persona helps to not only build a case for her womanist style of speech but also further demonstrates the way in which the womanist rhetor uses the conventional linguistic devices at her disposal in a manner that functions on her specific Black audience, whether held together by religious belief or extending toward political mobilization. While anaphora, amplification, and alliteration are easily heard throughout the body of the speech from the versions available, Chisholm's womanish wisdom is evident in the content of her speech.

Calling back to President Lincoln, she discursively demonstrates that her plans will follow in those footsteps to feature and liberate those who have been left out, ignored, shunned, and cast to the side. Her call to action "Give me your help in this hour." gives the audience a sense of responsibility and the ability to make the morally superior decision: choose her as their leader. The audience is not inactive, nor is it inadequate. By speaking beyond the white political commentators and listeners, she discursively forges through and asks her community members, Church members, and constituents to set their sights beyond the Bedford-Stuyvesant community and instead toward the White House. If they are to rekindle their faith in the American system, they must not "look in vain" as they had done in the past. They must accept the challenge with the challenger candidate and use their intelligence and smartness with political expediency, knowing they can no longer trust those who have lied and lingered in the spotlight too long.

Movement 1: Textual Reflection or Assessing the Reconstruction of the Spoken Word

Rhetorical devices, as outlined in traditional Aristotelian understandings of rhetoric, typically work toward persuading a public called upon and invited to be full members of the polis. They actively represent the experience of the rhetor speaking and are able to remain within common civility. This is not the case with Black candidates, much less with Black women. Chisholm, who spoke of writing political speeches for other candidates before her own run for office, mastered language and culture in a very particular way. Using counter-language and a womanist persona, Chisholm was able to craft speeches with rhetorical devices such as anaphora, amplification, and alliteration throughout her campaign announcement speech strategically and masterfully.

Although such rhetorical devices were seen in famous speeches of Reverend Martin Luther King Jr. and Malcolm X, Chisholm's command of these tools were utilized before a similar audience but operationalized beyond what they realized with a prophetic hope, coupled with a political tenor. Chisholm had to carefully and masterfully shape her speech to hold on to the responsibilities she maintained with her constituents, not only a divine entity. There is no doubt a semblance of the African American prophetic tradition shaped her perspective on Blackness and the responsibility politics must have in shaping the future opportunities of the Black community, for evil or for good. For example, in King's "I Have a Dream" speech, the words yet borrowed and originally branded by Reverend Prathia Hall, King's vibrato in 1963 at the March on Washington reverberates with the now well-memorized line. It simultaneously recalls his dream and provokes into the fiber of reality a prophecy that must come to pass. His hope was not actualized in his lifetime. Likewise, Chisholm passed away before seeing eventual president Barack Obama inhabit the White House. While comparable to King, a figure her Black audience remembers and others well knew, her use of anaphora and amplification function more similarly to Sir Winston Churchill's in his "We Shall Fight on the Beaches" speech. By subversively and skillfully, though silently, operationalizing tactics of celebrated orators, Chisholm demonstrates a particular facet of critical engagement in her speech making that a traditional analysis would miss.

As a rhetorical device, anaphora works by repeating a series of words consistently throughout a set of thoughts or ideas. The repetition of the word or set of words emphasizes ideological importance or something more. King consistently reminds his audience of his dream that paints a prophetic picture of liberating possibilities, not just for his children but for all "little girls and boys" to live and play together in peace and harmony. Some twenty-four years before, the world was in a state of war engaged in battles from nation to nation and field to field.

Unlike the Vietnam War of Chisholm's era, to which she was vehemently opposed, World War II posed a different and altogether more difficult set of responsibilities for leaders like Winston Churchill. After being invited to his alma mater, the Harrow School, on October 29, 1941, he spoke to the military academy students, teachers, and staff of the lessons learned from remaining tenacious, even with the threat of death, fear, and hopelessness. Famously stating, "Never give in. Never give in. Never, never, never, never—in nothing, great or small, large or petty—never give in, except to convictions of honour and good sense. Never yield to force. Never yield to the apparently overwhelming might of the enemy." By using anaphora in this situation, Churchill entreats a call of action, accountability, purpose, and perseverance into the hearts of the audience, though they may only see themselves as student's incapable of setting forth change upon the "darker days" ahead.

However, as this speech was set in the middle of World War II, Churchill pushes his audience to see that "darker days" are only "sterner days" that they can push toward and have the privilege to enhance and improve for the better. By using anaphora in these two circumstances, King and Churchill grapple with dark and gloomy realities. King is fighting against systemic racism against the Black community in a country unwilling to make well of its ideological promises of freedom, liberty, and justice. Churchill fights against the fascism that seems to be creeping across the European continent swiftly like a plague with no cure. What is imperative to note from these speeches is not necessarily the way they may have shaped the ideological or political perspective of her presidential campaign announcement speech but how they serve as an example of how anaphora is an effective rhetorical device that moves political audiences. Furthermore, Chisholm uses amplification to carry her use of anaphora throughout the entirety of her speech.

Amplification works in two ways in Chisholm's speech. Throughout the speech, she combines amplification in her text (or actual words) with her tone, pace, and speed. In his book *Writing with Clarity and Style: A Guide to Rhetorical Devices for Contemporary Writers*, Robert A. Harris (2017) outlines various definitions, examples, and rules for using rhetorical devices in speech and writing. He suggests, "Amplification involves repeating a word or expression while adding more detail to it, in order to emphasize what might otherwise be passed over. In other words, amplification allows you to call attention to, emphasize, and expand a word or idea to make sure the reader realizes its importance or centrality in the discussion" (para. 8). In the speech, Chisholm not only uses amplification in her content but also considers her tone and pace when she explains who she is and what her purpose will be, not only in the beginning of her announcement but through the entire speech. Harris explains, "Amplification can overlap with or include a repetitive device like anaphora when the repeated word gains further definition or detail" (para. 8). For example, by combining anaphora and amplification from the beginning, Chisholm states, "I am not the candidate of Black America, although I am Black and proud." In this first phrase, she repeats "I am" to clarify who she *is*, while carrying amplification into her phrase to further explain who she is *not*. In a similar example from his handbook, Harris entreats his readers to notice "the much greater effectiveness this repetition-plus detail form can have over a 'straight' syntax" (para. 8).

Beyond Chisholm, Churchill, or King, the use of anaphora and amplification are part and parcel to exploring religious texts within the Black preaching tradition. By amplifying or extending and emphasizing the meaning of a set of words, a phrase, or a particular theological construct, the preacher goes beyond high, holy homiletics and teaches the congregation how to interpret the text more thoroughly. Usually, amplification in this sense is heard in the second way Chisholm uses it, which focuses on the oral tradition of the Black political and religious audience. Audibly, her volume increases and decreases at particular moments to carry a point across and draw her audience into her words and ideas, underscoring a tonal shift mimetically marking the Black sacred desk from which she speaks. The rises and falls of Chisholm's voice function not simply as a great political orator but to carry with her the weight of the prophetic nature of the African American rhetorical tradition. Furthermore, her physical setting in a historic Black Church that was committed to social justice carries the weight of responsibility not simply to speak truth to power but to enact Micah 6:8, which calls the assembly to "go humbly and do justice in the name of [our] God." Despite any real theological or religious commentary being considered in her speech, the fact that Chisholm is standing within the Church and, no less, behind a pulpit, there is a certain way in which her speech moves the audience with audible clapping, cheering, and involvement. As such, the Black political audience is much like the Black religious audience through the Afrocentric practice of call-and-response. Early on, Chisholm is establishing her public counter to one of conventional construction.

Chisholm postures herself as a prolific political speechwriter and capable of captivating an audience, not simply through using rhetorical devices in which many are familiar but by skillfully combining others and remaining authentically tied to her Black audience, though it seems as though she rejects her Blackness and femininity, only to claim it haphazardly. However, this is not the case but instead a very intriguing exercise that demonstrates her discursive dexterity in front of a mixed, and highly critical, audience of those listeners who may not be a part of the intended group that can be trusted. When she says she is not the candidate for Black America, this remark is made because she is not a Black man. Subsequently, she is not the candidate for the women's movement, because she is not a white woman. She uses litotes, which reinforce a tactic that emphasizes a negative syntactical structure in order to emphasize an overarching point. Immediately, a reader well versed in traditional rhetorical devices would surmise that the construction of these sentences uses antithesis juxtaposing her situational reality with the nature of a society that yet would receive a Black woman as a front contender for president. While this assertion is correct, there is more to what Chisholm is doing here.

Chisholm then states, "I am not the candidate of any political bosses or fat cats or special interests." With clapping and cheers throughout her speech delivery, the audience gathered responds not simply to the words she uses but the very way she constructs her text. By using polysyndeton, or an excessive number of unnecessary conjunctions, she again stresses who she is by overemphasizing what she is *not*. In this way, Chisholm heads off her political competition, commentators, and doubters that would attack the legitimacy of her candidacy but positions herself as the underdog, or what Trent et al. (2011) deem the "challenger" candidate in political communication. According to Watkins-Dickerson and Johnson (2019), Chisholm knew well of her outsider status and used this to her advantage by adopting a womanist style in her speech. By trying to establish something new and fresh, by holding up the will, hopes, and dreams of the people, Chisholm stood apart from others in the field, beyond her race and gender.

Directly after she explains that she is a self-made and self-supported candidate, Chisholm uses apophasis. Apophasis functions by detaching the rhetor from demagogic behavior, particularly to set them apart as a moral exemplar. In this case, I contend Chisholm uses the challenger profile as an advantage. While society may render her body and voice invalid, she uses this particular rhetorical device to validate her and legitimize her campaign speech, as she explains she does not want to "offer to you the tired and glib clichés, which for too long have been an accepted part of our political life." Following this device, Chisholm cleverly applies apostrophe, reinvigorating the audience to rejoin her speech with "my fellow Americans." She reminds them that her aim is to not provide the common political soliloquy but to incite a new sort of conversation or dialogue for addressing the needs of the wider collective. Typically cast to the side, unheard, and lacking respect, this particular Black woman gives a political speech for the ages and paints herself as a political exemplar, a candidate anyone can trust, and a leader that holds high moral accord in her day-to-day responsibilities to the nation, over and against others that have delivered false hopes and promises.

As Chisholm speaks of the "deceit and deception" of the current administration, compressing her "d" and "c" consonants, which play very well to her slight lisp, she is allowing her sounds to carry a slight hiss at the crowd. While she does not shame the audience, she instead passively paints a picture that lacks integrity for the current political party in power and those who accept the lack of integrity. In this way, it could be argued that she considers they may hear what she is saying using alliteration but by once again poignantly positioning herself as a moral exemplar, and a Black woman still.

Finally, by using tricolon crescens, Chisholm increases her sentiments toward the necessity for better, more receptive leadership the American people can trust. Working to persuade her audience that new leadership will help them move forward, she appeals again to her audience. Chisholm says, "Americans, must demand stature and size in our leadership—leadership, which is fresh, leadership, which is open, and leadership, which is receptive to the problems of all Americans." Interestingly, the petite Chisholm builds her voice and persona beyond what is expected of her. With every word uttered, she casts aside the collective memory of Black women not having the ability to stand tall as prolific candidates in the American political system. As an American and as a public servant, Chisholm's rhetorical ethic demands civic participation and integrity among voters, and also within the halls of Capital Hill and the White House. Tricolon crescens, like a crescendo in music, builds the rhetorical progress of a stanza by repeating the same word over and over, demonstrating its importance. In this case, Chisholm complicates its definition by juxtaposing who holds the seat of power with those who should.

Movement 2: You're in the "Right Place"

Finding the right place to deliver the presidential announcement speech is a feat that surely takes time, effort, and a great deal of thought. Certainly, candidates consider their audience, but the actual setting or place of their first platform speech as a presidential contender is equally important. There has been little to no academic writing on presidential announcement speeches and the physical setting, but some considerations that may be important would include acoustics, aesthetic beauty, and even projecting an austere space reflecting the prolific office the contender hopes to inhabit. In a 2015 NPR.org article by Brakkton Booker, this idea is briefly considered. The title insists "How Candidates Announce Can Say a Lot About Their Campaigns," and certainly this is the case with Black women, as noted in this text. Booker considers the 2016 presidential candidates, beginning with the well-known former secretary of state and first lady Hillary Clinton. Although she was a household name, he suggests Clinton had a number of hurdles to overcome because she was, in fact, too austere or unapproachable, thus leaving her open to criticism for her lack of "touch" or commonality with the average voter. While Booker does not go into extensive detail considering terminology or theory relevant to the field of communication studies, he does suggest some important ideas about how candidates must pick the "right place" to build their presidential platform. This setting, in fact, shapes the backdrop of their intended audience. It also communicates who they are and where their political values are held. Although Congresswoman Chisholm was not noted as a member of the Church where she announced her presidential campaign, she made an important, strategic decision to share with the world her hopes and dreams for being commander in chief in the pulpit of a historically Black Church in Brooklyn, New York. This decision alone situated her speech as decidedly aligned with the Black community, whether or not she was the candidate for Black America or supported by the Congressional Black Caucus she helped charter only years prior.

Located at the historic Concord Baptist Church of Christ in her Bedford-Stuyvesant neighborhood, Chisholm delivered her speech in the presence of an enthusiastic audience cheering her on before she began delivering her speech. A number of press microphones lined the pulpit desk, at times slightly obstructing the camera view of Chisholm's petite frame. Visible still were the red liturgical linens placed upon the helm and common to many Protestant Christian churches. Despite some efforts of draping and technology to secularize the platform, the trained eye could easily make out the difference between this podium and others based plainly on these simple religious dressings. To her side, Black male preachers stood guard and in support of a woman they thought worthy to represent them in Congress and, quite possibly, as president of the United States. If nothing else, she was one of their own because during this time, a Black woman who was not a preacher or member of the Church would not always be welcome in the pulpit. This says a lot not only about Chisholm's political résumé but of her personal relationships. To stand exuding confidence, pride, excitement, and skill, along with the support of clergy and constituents alike, Shirley Chisholm was making more than a simple statement.

Even though most, if not all, political campaigns are made up of a wide array of news media, political commentators, and more, the physical setting of the place Chisholm chose was quite unique. As a traditional maker of hope, civility, and freedom in the Black community, the Black Church provides an essence a canonical ideological style cannot capture. This is because the space is not only a historically Black Church but at the time, Concorde was pastored by one of the most prolific pastors of the Black homiletics tradition.

In March of 1948, the Reverend Gardner Calvin Taylor became the pastor of Concord Baptist Church of Christ. Known as the dean of Black preaching, Taylor was a contemporary of Reverend Martin Luther King Jr. and worked tirelessly as a civil rights activist, teacher, preacher, and pastor within and outside of his Bedford-Stuyvesant neighborhood. As expressed in the contextualization section of this chapter, sharing space in the African American pulpit is not only a rare opportunity and set aside for those who have expressed a particular ministerial calling or prophetic gifting but is an honor to receive. For a preacher as noteworthy as Taylor to share or offer a space of this sort is certainly a concept that should not be overlooked or underevaluated. In fact, Taylor's history of preaching and his activism as it relates to Chisholm is not documented but in this moment speaks volumes to their shared values, similar faith ideals, and commitment to equitable politics.

Every place has a story, and every story begins in a particular place. By picking this specific setting of the Black Church, Chisholm is not only defining her style as womanist but demonstrating that a womanist rhetor purposely places herself in spaces that will appreciate, protect, and applaud her vision from a pulpit platform that speaks with integrity; reclaims life, liberation, and love; while also generating an audience to serve as a "living cloud of witnesses" to prophetic vision, political or otherwise. Because the setting of the Black Church holds a history filled with tragedy and triumph that only members of the African American community can fully embrace and understand, Chisholm's speech backdrop is decidedly different because of it. Although Chisholm skillfully remains neutral in her rhetoric surrounding race, she punctuates its importance by standing at the helm of a Black pulpit that engages with the African American religious audience Sunday after Sunday. Matching her intent for a womanist audience, which I discuss in "Movement 3," Chisholm creates a roadmap for Black women candidates to follow if they are committed to similar theological values, oral traditions, and everyday experiences.

Movement 3: Womanist Audience

In his book *Publics and Counterpublics*, Michael Warner (2002) considers the dynamics of what constitutes a communicative audience. Either by reading or hearing, members of a public are immediately enjoined in a communicative act, civic or otherwise. However, Warner's descriptions of what constitutes a public follow the linear neo-Aristotelian model that normatively sets certain prerequisites unattainable for marginalized individuals. Instead, theorizing between Arthur Smith's (later Molefe Asante) Black religious audience and Andre Johnson's African American audience provides a more accurate depiction of the audience of what could be a womanist rhetor. In his essay "The 'Scold of Black America': Obama, Race, and the African American Audience," Johnson explains that this group is activated and acquired by venerating the prophetic voice. This is not simple convergence toward the speaker itself but the agentive voice remains with the group. The people, as a collective, choose to hear, listen, act, and react to a voice that carries with it goodwill, wisdom, and exceptional integrity—or an individual that carries a prophetic ethos. Like the religious and faith traditions of the Black communities across the African diaspora, the audience or members of a Black public are constituted by a belief that the rhetor has been chosen by the community (or a higher power) and can speak on their behalf with righteousness, rightness, and decisiveness, and maintain their dignity. As such, the constitution of the Black audience follows the inverse of the five steps offered by Warner.

I argue that a *Black* public, or audience, is organized by a spirit of *in spite of*, as best heard in Maya Angelou's famous poem "Still I Rise" ([1978] 2013). In spite of anti-Black racism, the audience forms. In spite of 400 years of forced production, we collectively strive. In spite of a lack of dignity, humanity, and personhood afforded to us in current social conditions, police brutality, and systemic injustice in every institution, it is the indominable spirit that remains willing to remain attuned to the prophetic hope. This is not an eschatological yearning for relief from this world. It is an *in spite of* spirit that persistently resists and incessantly persists to be taken seriously, even if it means you are the *first*. While Warner contends that a public, in the normative sense, is said to be self-organized, it is "created by discourse itself" and nothing more (2002, 413). Conversely, a *Black* public is a relation among extended and/or fictive kin that share a relationship due to the phenomenological history of Blackness and their ontological situatedness within it. Granted, my goal in exploring the differences between normative publics and the Black audience is not to essentialize Blackness but instead to underscore the refusal to provide consistent benefits of citizenship to those that are othered and demonized, not by their character but by their race, class, and gender.

The address of a *Black* public speech is *always* personal, whereas Warner's third point argues that "the address of public speech is both personal and impersonal" (2002, 317). Certainly, neither Chisholm's speech nor the women who followed her directly dealt with each specific individual within earshot. Yet for those who had clear entry into the Black audience—well understanding its rules of interdependence, balance, harmony, social uplift, and the central value of community—her words called unto them. Their response to listen, only then, called the space into being something effective and operational. Thus, the imperative of a womanist audience includes biological and social relations and understands and holds on to the leadership vision cast by the Black woman at its helm. This follows the womanist tenet of traditional communalism, not simply in that the Black woman rhetor cares about her community but in that the community reciprocates support.

Warner's normative definition of a public is said to be "constituted through mere attention" (2002, 419). This is neither the case for a Black audience, nor is it so for a womanist audience. Whether the Black man or woman is listening to the speech or not, he or she can and will be effected and affected. Simply being present in the collective calls together a spirit of rise and fall, purpose and push toward a community agenda. It is a sort and sense of active listening that requires response, as can be heard by the cheers, claps, and callbacks as Chisholm projects her agenda for the presidency. This aspect of community and collectivity is inherently tied to the identity of Blackness, and womanist rhetors understand the rise and fall of call-and-response. She identifies the personal struggles she has shared and the particular schedule for change she is preparing, outlining her message buttressed by prophetic intention. For example, Bass's vice-presidential acceptance speech demonstrates this by considering the history of bondage imposed upon African Americans and those of the wider African diaspora. Referring to the widely understood Exodus passage when she says her theme for the campaign is "let my people go," one need not be in hearing distance. There is also no need to read or attend to exact references of this passage to be positively and politically affected. Again, hearing in the collective creates agency, and the story, while public, still reaches toward personal experience of captivity, or a collective memory of it. Whether sacred or secular, rhetoric shared in the space of a Black collective still exists and moves within the "souls of Black folk." Having the opportunity and the option to be "let go" contends with the mental, emotional, political, economic, educational, and spiritual strongholds slavery and its aftermath of Jim/Jane Crow, racism, and white supremacist policies. Bass's speech prophetically leans into and Chisholm's potential to provide some semblance of hope against those superimposed upon societal confines, constraints, and conditions of the Black body.

The womanist audience has all of the elements of the *Black* public, as briefly described, yet its ability to reclaim attention and agency through the voice of a Black woman rhetor standing in the face of white patriarchy makes it unique. This distinct difference decisively dismantles demonizing normative discourse against misogynoir. As the central voice and embodied presence of the prophetic message going forth to speak to the community, such a challenge to the communicative cannon poses danger and is positioned as an active threat to the status quo, when in fact it could very well be the prophetic "balm in Gilead" all are hoping to receive. In this way, Chisholm's audience naturally amplifies her words through the agency they provide and attention they maintain. Reclaiming attention and agency proactively breaks down normative barriers toward the road ahead of the rhetor and galvanizes her to enter into new discursive territory. Though uncharted for Chisholm, the active buy-in of her audience, as evidenced by their engagement, signifies a clear chasm in how Black and white spaces are normed and formed, hence analyzing them from different perspectives allows readers and hearers to receive distinct byproducts of the speech event. More importantly, as the Black and womanist audience is formed through the collective, and not simply by speech itself, we are able to identify how power is rationed and shared among the group. Chisholm would not have been able to obtain this response, let alone entry into this space, without genuine relationship. Collective energy without connection is a normative cause, whereas the womanist audience is curated through integrity. Chisholm was not only able to stand within the hall of a Black Church and use counterlanguage to craft a gifted speech. Her previous work laid the foundation to galvanize a community to accept her as a candidate. The community responded, lending their voices and ears to her cause. Chisholm was seen and valued as one worthy of being supported, not simply for what she promised for the future or her résumé but her historical presence as a proven member of the community in which she lived and was formed.

Movement 4: Coming to Voice.

The power and command for language is important for how we see speech in general, and womanist speech, in particular. Reverend Taylor George (2015) explains, "Words not only convey meaning; they embody reality. Through the power of the Spirit, the preacher's words make present in time things that are separated in space, the realities of judgment and mercy, origins and end, paradise and perdition" (para. 7). To this extent, because the Black political audience is arguably born of the Black preaching sphere (Christian and non-Christian), the womanist political candidate must not only speak truth to power. She must also possess an inherent fortitude toward linguistic artistry, honesty, prophetic fire, and wit. Said another way, ethos must not be established in seeking individualistic affirmations, which follow the model of Western capitalism, but must seek the confirmation and consternation of the *Black* public itself. With this in mind, "coming to voice" means that the speaker not only knows who she is but what she is capable of doing, and is focused on achieving it to the best of her ability. Therefore, when a womanist rhetor comes to voice her agency is communally raised and maintained by her consistently persistent relationship with the community that upholds her calling. Chisholm comes to voice in a historically Black Church made up of a live studio audience of Black men and women as her main support. Even in her response to questions from the media after she finishes her speech, she maintains a rhetorical persona that, on the surface, fits the ideas and ideals of white individuals in the audience but works and serves the tongue and cheek response well known in Black rhetorical circles as "playing the dozens." When asked about whether she is worried her candidacy will take away votes from the current mayor, she responds by saying that they are both trying to gain support in the same area. Better yet, "He should be worried" about her votes and not Chisholm!

Met with a roar of laughter from the audience, and a visibly responsive Reverend Taylor (who is on the left of Chisholm in the pulpit), Chisholm is not only witty but quickly fends off contention and challenge about the legitimacy of her candidacy. She stands firmly within the agency offered to her by the audience surrounding her, holding on to it with pride and precision and purpose. She maintains her position as a threat and viable contender. Although she makes it clear that most of the mainstream politicians and donors are not backing her financially or politically, the confidence she displays articulates radically redemptive self-love. This womanist tenet is made even more powerful with her community displaying active support and feedback. The moments of call-and-response do not end just because the announcement speech is complete. Instead, the audience acknowledges her presence and cleverly sharp responses with laughter, clapping, and facial expressions of excitement. They not only "get the joke" but accept her as one of their own. Interestingly, this is the moment when footage from the video becomes distorted, and it is difficult to analyze the remaining conversation and questions momentarily.

In spite of the fact that coming to voice as a womanist rhetor begins with validating the self, the Black community, made up of both women and men, must also validate each other. This is primarily important in order to ensure the circle of faith, hope, and the liberative ethic of collectivism is achieved together. This is not necessarily the case within traditional rhetorical constructs, nor is it part and parcel of a feminist rhetorical theory. Yet it is true for Chisholm as a womanist rhetor, from my summation. Her womanist style is not compromised or neutralized due to her statements that refer to "the

American people" or "women" in general but are potentially made stronger because she realizes the need for a public persona in the physical body in which she exists. More than this, exacting who she is and the pride in her identity arguably make her more capable and competent. Her audience not only agrees that she is better able to speak across and beyond her Blackness and femininity. Overall, the multiple standpoints she is forced to live within and be confined to remain give her a very particular set of parameters as she comes to voice. As she finds herself, amid the *in spite of* spirit, her voice as a candidate for the president of the United States remains one of the benchmarks to follow for women (and others) running for political office, especially if they are the *first*.

CONCLUSION

Exactly one hundred years after Victoria Woodhull positioned herself as the first female presidential candidate, Chisholm pushed the envelope even further. Only two years after the passing of the Fourteenth Amendment, Woodhull's 1872 campaign began the establishment of a rhetorical persona for women in politics, displaying the ways in which the larger society rejected their candidacy, based solely on their femininity. Ellen Fitzpatrick's (2016) text *The Highest Glass Ceiling* describes the ways in which society quipped and quoted Woodhull's rhetorical persona, affectively rejecting her candidacy as preposterous and pretentious. Unlike Chisholm, Woodhull did not have the benefit of a generation of women voting before her infamous charge toward the presidency. Yet Chisholm's experience of sexism and misogyny cannot be discounted nor compared to the difficulties experienced by Woodhull. This is primarily due to the advantages of whiteness afforded to Woodhull and the disadvantages of Blackness guaranteed by Chisholm's raced, gendered, and classed positionality in a society primarily valuing Black women's bodies in historical tropes outside of leadership and esteem.

Whereas Woodhull and Chisholm made history during traumatic times, their experiences had interesting similarities and extreme difference. Because both candidates were women, they experienced the difficulties sexism and misogyny offered them in a land ruled by patriarchal conventions and ideals. In Chisholm's time and especially in the nineteenth century, the ideals of Victorian womanhood crafted an image of femininity confining women to the roles of wives and mothers. This meant women were expected to be supportive of the men they married and the children they bore. Women were rarely legal landowners, and they were not able to vote. This image was still buttressed well into the 1970s, even with the rising of the women's liberation movement. Yet anti-Black racism, in particular, reinforced this reality for Black women.

While white women did not particularly enjoy the pushes and pulls patriarchal standards forced against their voices and bodies inside and outside of the domestic realm, Black women were suffering from the economic, educational, political, and class struggles their femininity guaranteed them and their race further complicated. As such, Black women are described as experiencing more than a double bind or Du Bois's double consciousness (1903). As King describes, multiple factors attack their consciousness exhibited in the classed experiences of racism and sexism.

As an individual of reasonable financial means, Woodhull's political exposure and education far surpassed many other women of her day and time. The fact that she was a woman proved to be an uncompromising "double bind" for her campaign and the way in which the American public refused to receive her as a candidate (Fitzpatrick 2016). More than this, her ability to exist within a social caste that allowed white women of status to come to voice and disavowed Black men and women the vote made her campaign distinctive. However, it was yet absent still of the particular challenges Chisholm would have to face years down the road. Four decades before the Twentieth Amendment, though her virtuosity may have been contested, her womanhood and femininity were not. Her contest toward the presidency as divorcee, spiritualist, and polyamorous broker of the first Wall Street firm owned by a woman was a notable achievement for her day. Woodhull's run for the presidency was remarkable, and many scholars may consider her a protofeminist, yet her personal and political trials, while made distinct by her gender, only scratch the surface of the plight of Black women's political endeavors, as a whole, in the American arena of government.

All in all, Chisholm follows a womanist style that shapes a way to understand rhetorical criticism outside of the monotonous and at times bellicose analytical tools generally accepted. By extending Johnson's (2015) womanist rhetorical criticism into four movements, I argue that Congresswoman Shirley Chisholm not only crafted a womanist rhetorical genre (Watkins-Dickerson and Johnson 2019) but also provided a blueprint for other Black women to follow in political communication. By considering her speech script and oral performance, looking closely at the text for conventional rhetorical devices met with counterlanguage, Chisholm's setting and audience allow her to come to voice in a space that profits and protects Black women's ideals and values.

Chapter 4

"Defining Myself... Is One of the Most Difficult Challenges I Face"
The Presidential Campaign Announcement Speech of Senator Carol Mosley Braun

> It's *not* impossible for a woman—a Black woman—to become President.
> —CAROL MOSELY BRAUN

Black feminist scholars Gloria T. Hull, Patricia Bell-Scott, and Barbara Smith (1982) explain, "The political position of Black women in America has been, in a single word, embattled" (xvii). Black women's beginnings in this country were tied to tales of servitude instead of scholastic depth, leaving the attention and acknowledgment of their intellectual productivity unstudied. It still needs more attention to the embattled nature of their political lives and grows beside the complex nature of how this text investigates womanist rhetoric in the presidential announcement speeches of Shirley Chisholm, Carol Moseley Braun, and Kamala Harris. In large part, their politics, in spite of the challenges surrounding their communicative acts, is very productive. However, to be viewed as productive embraces a political nature. This politic of productivity surrounds Black women in several different ways. Historically, it has been measurable primarily by the profitability of their reproductive and productive labor. Simplified to mean that their silenced bodies are what is measured as profitable because of what they can do and how they can perform for others. Black women are neither seen as members of the polis nor invited into the neo-Aristotelian measure of what constitutes a public.

Hull et al. (1982) continue by clarifying, "The extremity of our oppression has been determined by our very biological identity. The horrors we have faced historically and continue to face as Black women in a white male-dominated society have implications for every aspect of our lives" (xvii–xviii). While there has been much improved research highlighting their speeches and doing analysis of the words they say, truly delving into the inner weavings of those words from a theoretical perspective has not been the consistent project of most political communication scholarship. Thus, my use of womanist rhetorical criticism seeks to highlight, not simply a line by line analysis of their speeches but a larger consideration of the links between the speeches of Black women. The overarching thematic rhetorical movements they re-create based on the epistemological privilege they carry into the presidential announcement speeches they share do not only say a great deal about society. Their speeches say even more about the links they share as women who dare to believe *anything* is possible.

Consequently, for Carol Elizabeth Moseley Braun to speak and to believe (even if just for a moment) that a Black woman should run for president and *could* be commander in chief, there exists the evidence and reach of prophetic discourse within the wider African American rhetorical tradition. This was a tradition that was embraced by the historical candidacy of Shirley Chisholm. It shows a Black woman in tune with herself and her ability to extend such powerful and thought-provoking words beyond her present state and stature, both physical and political. When considering Moseley Braun, womanist rhetorical theory can be understood not merely as *prophetic* but also as *practical*.

Extending Hull et al.'s definition of "brave" may provide space to grasp Moseley Braun's rhetorical persona throughout her speech. However, I deem a more formidable term is necessary to depict Moseley Braun as a political candidate and communicator. I argue that her radically redemptive self-love extended in a future possibility is best described by the term "womanist," directly from Alice Walker's definition. She says, "A womanist is Responsible. In charge. Serious. Womanist is to feminist as purple is to lavender" (xi–xii). Women that are not only prophetic but practical are in charge. They can manage leaders. These women, Black women, are not simply the best alternative but are the answer to many of society's ills. There is a deeper hue to her strength; a deeper strength in her discourse. But unfortunately, there is a deeper discursive gymnastic she must demonstrate, all while being prophetic, in tune with herself and her community, and critically aware enough to save her life and those of others who are to come.

For a political contender to be prophetic, she must be in a league of her own. For a presidential candidate to be practical, however, she must be charging forth with a sense of "realness," pragmatism, and concern that is based on garnering results, not simply on distant promises that have yet to be realized. She must say and consider that it *is* possible for a Black woman to become president of the United States. "Practical" is the word Carol Moseley Braun used to describe herself and her campaign during her announcement speech. While the word itself was only used three times, it deserves mention because it transforms the typical caricatures of irrationality, impracticality, and impossibility Black womanhood is assumed on its head, hoping to transcend into the prophetic reach of Chisholm's vision, and the entire African American race's long-held dream. Because of the sociohistorical precedent of Black women's political reality in the modern era, Black women being in charge of their sense of self, voice, body, and political aspirations has been believed to be *impractical*. However, Moseley Braun and the Black women of this study, strive for something strikingly different, with a drive, defiance, and hermeneutic of self-determination unparalleled by many of their peers. Not only this but the idea that Moseley Braun is practical and expresses her character to be tempered and thoughtful automatically casts others in the presidential race as impractical, or even inept. Of course, she is not only exemplifying one of the characteristics of counterlanguage but signifying beyond the range of her mixed audience.

In this chapter, I will detail her presidential announcement speech by considering the ways in which she worked out the probability of winning and the practicality of the Black and female positionality against the patriarchal thrust of white supremacy, militarism, expansionism, neoimperialism, and terrorism. But more than this, Moseley Braun's sentiments toward being a practical choice for a seemingly impossible campaign demonstrate how womanist rhetorical theory does not simply function within the molds of being a strategically prophetic discursive model but one that is also built in practical, sensible, calculated terms that are derived from the womanist tenet of critical engagement. Yet what holds Moseley Braun, along with the others, back is the understanding that Black women are not only cast as impractical because of the multiple jeopardy they experience but the ways in which this jeopardy creates a multiple consciousness and the ethos society refuses to offer their voice.

In analyzing Moseley Braun's speech, I will continue to utilize womanist rhetorical theory to consider the application of *practical* discursive decisions Moseley Braun made in her presidential announcement speech, as well as in the construction of her overall rhetorical persona. Though her choices, demeanor, and background were similar and different than Chisholm, Moseley Braun's statements, positions on the issues, and carefully crafted embodied discourse construct a particular presence demonstrating her clear understanding of how to garner success on a national stage, particularly as a Black woman. I consider what I call the "politics of practicality" alongside womanist rhetorical criticism in the speech analysis, while working to chart another actualized space for the womanist rhetor: as practical politician. I consider the ways in which practicality can persuade the unpersuadable audience at best and, at worst, distance them even further. I will also consider the ways in which it is not only different from what is known as "political correctness" but also take note of the embodied discursive tenets Black women must strategize when taking this stance as a speaker.

"I AM PRACTICAL": MOSELEY BRAUN AND THE POLITICS OF PRACTICALITY

Traditionally, all candidates use their presidential announcement speech as an opportunity to persuade their audience of their ability to win, spark change, or remain steadfast as a moral exemplar for the country and for the world. Yet there is much to say about what Moseley Braun could mean and the inherent profundity and promise of her use of the word "practical." Again, my goal for this project is to identify the theoretical frames and forming themes developing within womanist rhetoric over anything else. Usual proscriptions and assumptions, while at times helpful, are not wholly acceptable in how we should understand the candidates within this text. Therefore, when Moseley Braun says she is "practical," she is saying more than what meets the ear at the surface of her message. Being "practical" and being "the practical choice" for the presidency was one of the key words/phrases strategically emphasized in Moseley Braun's presidential campaign announcement speech.

However, functioning outside of the normative communication cannon in order to provide a rhetorical analysis, I suggest Moseley Braun is doing more than this. As she speaks of her practicality, not only is she making ardent appeals to her audience about her fitness of intellect, will, decision-making ability, and leadership, but she is striving to shift the normative gaze that says Black women are impractical while also calling her opponents, particularly the incumbent, incapable and ineffectual. She makes mention of this passively and with tempered emotion. Yet the trained womanist ear reads between her words and sees the ways in which she demonstrates her ability to be rhetorically adroit. This skill, in turn, uplifts the womanist tenet of critical engagement. Certainly, membership has its privileges and the audience lends its ear to hear. From this position of her speech, we, specifically as listeners, are made aware that to be presidential, *typically and traditionally* means one must be practical. I would venture the definition she is considering of what makes a leader "practical" is an inherent ability to decipher between wise and irrational choices. More than this, a leader must have a tempered, steady nature. Thus, presidential practicality and political possibility for Black women are best suited to those whose rhetorical positioning denies them the opportunity for easy choices. To be presidential, "staying alive" and remaining steady in the midst of trouble are character traits brought on by a liberative ethos that is consistent through turmoil and triumph. It is the inherent trait of integrity, character, virtue, and even piety as a subject, citizen, and rhetor. By claiming this for herself as the practical presidential candidate, Moseley Braun presents herself as morally superior. This is not because of the pain she has pushed through due to her race, gender, or class, but it is the *in spite of* spirt she maintains through it.

Despite the hardship, pain, and turmoil that has historically been our lot, Black women, like Moseley Braun, have believed they can rise above their social, historical, political, and economic circumstance. And *in spite of* such barriers, Black women have had the strength to dispel the myths holding their voices hostage. For instance, Maria Stewart was one of the first Black women to give public social speeches, leaving copies of her manuscripts. On September 21, 1832, Stewart spoke at Franklin Hall in Boston, Massachusetts, leaving with her audience the now infamous words "Why sit ye here and die?" calling her audience to take political action against slavery, poverty, and injustice (Blackpast 2007). She calls to their attention the need to understand that "few white persons of either sex, who are calculated for anything else, are willing to spend their lives and bury their talents in performing mean, servile labor" (Blackpast 2007). Her words were not shared to demean those relegated to service industry work but to provoke and persuade Black men and women to see the far-reaching possibilities and intellectual capability they had to move beyond their social stagnation. In this and many instances, the political stage is the throne upon which such implications for hope, camaraderie, change, and equality are cast, voted for, and tallied to steer the future in a better direction. Yet in the American context, the political narrative centers Black women's bodies and voices as irreverent and irrelevant. Such conclusions portray copiously violent religious discourses casting lots against their piety and capability, leaving false accounts of their personhood. These discursive exigencies serve as judge, jury, executioner, and publicity assistant, while also buttressing beliefs that fall upon the backs of the *least of these* to overcome without aid or apology. Therefore, Stewart obliges her listeners to raise girls with respectability, dignity, and class. Stewart compels her audience by saying, "Let our girls possess what amiable qualities of soul they may; let their characters be fair and spotless as innocence itself" (Blackpast 2007). This understanding of the self and hope for the self-actualized and well formed, goes beyond general respectability politics as we typically understand it to be. It also delves into a culture of dissemblance, hoping to be buried within the sacred and secret rhetorical safety of an embodied discourse that not only is safe from systemic harm but is seen as whole, right, true, and efficacious. Historian Darlene Clark Hine explains that a culture of dissemblance "enabled the creation of positive alternative images of their sexual selves and facilitated Black women's mental and physical survival in a hostile world" (1989, 920).

Taking Hine's lead, a politics of practicality can be defined as communicative command of traditional rhetorical rules and devices to be used to signify meaning beyond meaning, place beyond place, and law beyond law. This is to say that when Carol Moseley Braun repositions herself as the most practical candidate for the American presidency, she is saying that not only is she the best person for the job but she is the only candidate worthy, wise, and willful enough to get the job done with justice, integrity, and a sound mind. *In spite of* the fact Black women have been cast as morally depraved in television, history, and through political conjecture, Moseley Braun offers new meaning to old meaning; speaks steadfastly in a place built specifically for those not welcomed elsewhere; and stands morally righteous, not simply as a professional but in a prophetic manner by claiming authority over herself. Her confidence in her ability to work with any and everyone on such a high platform, calm, cool, collected, and voted as "the conscience of the house" should have garnered more attention than it did then, and certainly even today.

PRESIDENTIAL PRACTICALITY, POLITICAL POSSIBILITY, AND THE POSITION OF ETHOS FOR BLACK WOMEN

In the available political communication literature, focus on presidential campaign rhetoric is sparse and scant. Additionally, little analysis of the style, language, and persuasive techniques of African Americans in general and Black women in particular give us a glimpse of their discursive trials and triumphs in the political sphere. Because Black women and men have had difficulties pushing forward in state and national politics in comparison to their white counterparts, their speeches and campaigns have not gained analogous academic attention. The manner in which Black women and men speak and the rhetorical devices they use to craft persuasive arguments for their respective audiences is sparse. However, of the 162 African American members of the US Congress, only forty-seven of them have been women at the time of this text. Even when Black women are named, readers must note their identity beyond their femininity particularly due to the erasure of their racial reality and the particular constraints it can have on their effectiveness on the political stage.

Serving the state of Illinois from 1992 to 1998 as a US senator, Moseley Braun's smile and stamina amid her short stature made headlines across her state and around the nation during her political career. There are a number of news outlets that have captured her story, voice, and perspective. Some have celebrated Moseley Braun as a trailblazer with many "firsts." Others have unearthed the griminess of politics and the controversy of being in the public eye. Yet in blazing this path, the rhetorical fragments, interviews, essays, and her announcement speech offer a long-lasting impression of the ways we can work to understand Black women's political communication and womanist rhetorical theory. More than this, Moseley Braun, in fact, was just as qualified as any other candidate, as she confidently remarked during a PBS interview aired on May 24, 2010, titled "DuSable to Obama: Chicago's Black Metropolis." Yet she also alludes to the difficulty of her candidacy, not based on a lack of training or preparedness for campaigning but because of the hitches of historical womanhood and even racism. Underneath the surface, she is speaking of the difficulty Black women have in constructing ethos for audiences outside of their traditional sphere.

The Impracticality of Feminist Style for Womanist Rhetorical Theory

Modern and contemporary conceptions of ethos do not follow new rules or extensively expand the reach of the definition because it is yet embedded in its classical origins. For instance, textbooks such as Porrovecchio and Condit's *Contemporary Rhetorical Theory* (2016) are coded by the lack of sociolinguistic exploration within them and only serve a particular population and perspective. The writers suggest the purpose of the compilation of readings is "to provide a brief introduction to the contemporary issues and concerns that have animated the work of rhetorical theorists since the late 1960s—a time of great social, political, and intellectual change" (1–2). The authors admit their focus is on "the classical rhetorical perspective," which in many circles is read as neo-Aristotelian and white. With this in mind, Black women (and the communities they love) become sidelined through the consideration of "all the women" and "all the Blacks" in what can now be called the unfortunate truth in the chorus of Hull et al.'s text.

Sociologist Wini Breines (2002) explains that even as the civil rights movement antiwar campaign among activists outraged by Vietnam brought white and Black feminists together, it also made clear the differences, even in what is known as the contemporary age. In fact, she explains that while she originally conceived there to be no ideological differences between her and other white feminist activists during the 1960s and beyond, looking back, she realized her immediate assumption was not as developed as it is now. She says:

> Characteristically for a person of my race, class, and generation, I had attributed too much power to activists, including white and black feminists, and their abilities to reverse American racism in a few short years. I had believed the words of the civil rights anthem, "We Shall Overcome" (and "black and white together"), as had the white civil rights volunteers, that we could build an interracial feminist community quickly and without too much pain. Individual commitment appeared to be enough. I learned that capitalism, racism, and sexism are much more powerful than we were. In that chastening lesson, activists began to understand that racism is not only about individual belief but that it is a political, economic, and cultural system that shapes us all. We came face-to-face with enormous forces that were not only "out there" but were, despite our best intentions, inside of us. (Breins 2002, 1125–26)

Taking this testimony beside Moseley Braun's, it becomes more clear that Black women's voices are not only crowded out by explicit power of heteropatriarchal political tradition but also through the passivity of white women, who do not see (or see too late) the history of race and gender based oppression compiled together have a powerful effect on Black women and their ability to move outside of such constraints.

Sometimes due to misunderstanding, misappropriation, and mismanagement of power, Black women's voices are scant. When they are observed, the eventual whitewashing within the middle-class feminist voice far too often drowns out the particularities of their narrative voice, style, and story. It is mistakenly assumed that the feminist voice can and will be an admirable advocate for their survival and thriving; yet the feminist movement has often overemphasized women's shared experience while underemphasizing their benefit from anti-Blackness. As a result of this, the interconnectedness of Black women's political disenfranchisement and the amount of tension their truths produce for the profit of experiencing liberation creates a chasm within feminist theory. In our case, this generalizability of contemporary rhetorical theory can be highly problematic and incorrectly sift through the connective tissue of Black women's political narrative. To this end, political communication from a womanist perspective, therefore, brings ease toward considering Moseley Braun and the other women considered within this study, beginning not from a (white) feminist gaze but from a womanist one, even if she does not explicitly define herself through any critical theoretical construct.

For example, Kathleen E. Kendall's (1995) *Presidential Campaign Discourse: Strategic Communication Problems*, "focuses on communication problems in the 1992 presidential campaign, and the strategies candidates used to solve them" (ix). In the sole chapter primarily dedicated to specific issues of women, Suzanne Daughton (1995) briefly mentions the late congresswoman Barbara Jordan. Whereas 1992 was deemed the "Year of the Woman," six women were voted to represent their states and districts in Congress. One of those women was Carol Moseley Braun. She was the only African American senator, male or female, at that time. However, her name and the specialness of her victory are not explicitly mentioned, nor is any real conversation about race, ethnicity, or identity. Erasure and e-racing Black women from public memory can be a function and facet of highlighting feminist ideologies and methodologies, particularly when (only) gender is at the forefront of the debate.

While Daughton's chapter, "Women's Issues, Women's Places," deals with the reality of women being relegated to the domain of home, family, caretaker, and more, she mentions feminine ways of communicating in political spaces. Through Jordan, she says the hopes and dreams of women to (at some point) see and experience a woman in the White House was a powerful statement during her speech at the Democratic Convention. Daughton utilizes the feminist rhetorical framework of Karlyn Kohrs Campbell, particularly from *Man Cannot Speak for Her* (1989). To look deeper into Campbell's work, "feminine style" is used to distinguish and analyze these women. Furthermore, as it relates to Jordan's hope for a woman to be president, she explains her forthrightness in sharing that this wish was possible because she "had very little to lose by being so outspoken" (230). This is not simply a swift generalization of seniority releasing a Black congresswoman from rhetorical constraints of her ontological station. In but a few words, Campbell's analysis haphazardly disassociates Jordan's race and gender as dually categorized, caricatured, and classed elements of her identity. She both effectively and affectively negates and nullifies the reality of her voice as a Black woman in politics. Black women, no matter the prominence or political position they are promoted to, are *always* and *already* "missin' something" in relation to power, stability, voice, and safety (Shange 1997, 84). This brief, blundering statement erases and e-races the complexity of Jordan's voice, even in that moment.

The erasure and e-racing of Black women in politics through using feminist theory—as opposed to womanist, Black feminist, and other ideological perspectives aligned or loosely tied to Afrocentric ways of being—creates scholarship that misses the full mark of a person's ontological reality. While no ideological standpoint can rightly or righteously cover the whole of a person, omitting the racialized experience in favor of heteropatriarchal constructs of rank and tenure in American political space is a substantial oversight. Such considerations demonstrate the need to use other, more adequate analytical tools for scholars working to unearth the vision, value, and virtue of Black women's rhetoric. The fact that the very woman she misses is the first Black woman to be elected to the Senate and second African American in history is an incredible feat that highlights issues that any practical woman would consider. The tendency to sweep away Black women's words, wisdom, wit, experience, and the exigencies that collude against them in public and private spaces leaves political communication scholarship scant and in need of a womanist interjection.

To take this further, Phillis Wheatley and Belinda Sutton are two eighteenth-century Black women whose voices (and by extension bodies) are placed on trial, unwillingly silenced by the rhetorical constraints cast upon the bodily intersection in which they existed. Wheatley's trial challenges her abilities and poetic genius, while Sutton works to get her due from the estate of the master who enslaved her. While both women have some modicum of success in their cases, their agency is rendered just as invisible without the help and defense and advocacy of white sympathizers. Without the help, financial backing, and written skill of others, surely their voices and bodies stifled, demeaned, silenced, and doubted. Back then and even now, Black women are rendered silent. Berry and Gross (2020) explain: "African American women have remained underprotected and overpoliced, beginning with colonial laws that treated them as things rather than human beings, to more recent disparities that rendered them largely ignored victims of the War on Drugs and mass incarceration. Yet as Black women served lengthy prison sentences, they made demands on the state for justice" (211). Thus, the example of Wheatley and Sutton only opens the door toward demonstrating that feminine style (particularly from an *only* white feminist lens) is not a viable rhetorical option for Black women and should not be applied even in political settings where tenure is assumed a protective cloak.

Similarly with Moseley Braun, the refusal of rhetorical space for Black women due to their existence and experience within multiple intersections, jeopardies, realities, oppressions, and rhetorical quandaries leave them lifting, climbing, and venturing to leave unscathed but still carrying purpose. Due to this, understanding Moseley Braun's speech in its context, for its time, and based on the complex rhetorical situatedness of Black women who came before her requires us to think of Moseley Braun's speech and short campaign differently. Tracking her speech through a womanist rhetorical lens proves more beneficial than Campbell's feminist rhetorical style primarily because Moseley Braun is a Black woman. Additionally, womanism offers a theoretical beginning and end framed and offered by Black women to appropriately judge themselves and adequately call into existence their audience. Understanding the symbolism of hair, voice, dress, audience, tone, and even something as simple as a smile communicates something very different for Moseley Braun than it later would for former secretary Hillary Clinton. Shifting away from feminist style and considering womanist rhetorical style instead, I argue Moseley Braun's content is built by the several superimposed phenomenological pretexts shifting the eventual text she creates from the cultural context that shapes her. This predicament is commonly shared by many Black women in some manner, whether delivering a political speech, preaching, lecturing, or otherwise crafting a communicative act in public (and private) space. Thus, Senator Moseley Braun's goal to painstakingly point her narrative persona as practical is a rhetorical strategy of her own making but undeniably clever and *womanish*. Even though this persona may have been historically and politically impossible on a presidential stage, like Chisholm, she was fighting to win.

CONTEXTUALIZATION OF CAROL MOSELY BRAUN

Born in 1947 Chicago, Moseley Braun's education focused primarily on political science and law, paving the way for her journey in civic service. Her career in law and politics began as a prosecutor for the US attorney's office in Chicago. After being voted into the Illinois House of Representatives she rose to assistant majority leader. While in this position, her political activism was celebrated due to her work against racist laws that disproportionately affected African Americans and Hispanics. According to some accounts, Moseley Braun sought national office after incumbent Democratic senator Alan Dixon voted to confirm Justice Clarence Thomas. This could have possibly demonstrated her solidarity in response to Anita Hill's testimony amid the scandal of Thomas's sexual misconduct. Other testimony suggests she ran building on the quality work she completed as the recorder of deeds, and the push from her community to move further into the political sphere. In her first and only term in Congress, Moseley Braun spoke out against racism and the passivity of her white colleagues. As remarked in her presidential announcement speech, she was voted "the conscience of the House" for the state of Illinois in 1987, which was the same year she became the recorder of deeds in Cook County, Illinois. She served as ambassador to New Zealand under President William Clinton from December 1999 to March 2001. Regardless of the actual push toward seeking presidential service, Moseley Braun rose as a viable contender for the Democratic nomination with a résumé that matched her ability to serve as a practical leader.

Although her elusive list of experiences should have displayed her integrity and capability within her campaign performance and as a senator, establishing ethos or political credibility was difficult for Moseley Braun. Because she was a Black woman, her voice was inherently devalued. Celeste Walls (2004) argues in her essay "You Ain't Just Whistlin' Dixie: How Carol Moseley Braun Used Rhetorical Status to Change Jesse Helms' Tune" that Moseley Braun's social, personal, and rhetorical status were not only denigrated, devalued, and dismissed during the debate surrounding Amendment 610, which surrounded controversy regarding a patent to be issued for the United Daughters of the Confederacy but used against her as a valuable politician. At first, Helms, who was a senior member of Congress, used his inherently elevated status to outwit Moseley Braun and others by sliding the amendment into an otherwise unrelated vote. Without quick notice from Moseley Braun's staff while she was working in another committee meeting and cool thinking from Moseley Braun herself, the amendment would have passed without the blink of an eye by the all-white Senate. Walls explains that the first round of debate did not necessarily win Moseley Braun support but by centering herself, her privilege of perspective, she persuaded her audience to reconsider their vote and their own integrity.

The ideas Moseley Braun carried into her political platform for the presidency were not built in a vacuum, and I would argue that her initial thought process toward practicality and poise as major touchstones were instigated during her tenure as a congresswoman in the Senate. Indeed, this was built upon not only the experience of a woman who marched with Dr. King in her hometown of Chicago, Illinois, as a little girl, but also a stage curated by a woman who was raised amid the nuclear arms race and a nation at war with others and itself. As Black women are not typically thought to be "practical," Moseley Braun explains herself to be so during her presidential campaign announcement speech. Since the term "practical," in and of itself, connotes a sense of being businesslike, efficient, sensible, and sober minded, the way in which Black women's character has not historically been personified in this way matters incredibly. On the contrary, they have been unfailingly caricatured and/or characterized in terms and tenors that demonstrate how their discourse is lined with lewd and licentious behavior or is lazy and loud.

In 2004, the war on terror was a current campaign most Democrats were hoping to strategically work against. The Bush II presidency also gave a glimpse of political oligarchy and international instability crafted in a war on ideals and unproven or at least inconsistent allegations leaning toward imperialist tendencies. Amid a pool of male candidates, Moseley Braun's use of political civility in the midst of turmoil, confusion, war, and civil unrest allowed her to speak toward the exigence of war and political disorder, but as a Black woman she did not necessarily profit from this stance, nor did she gain masses of support from other women or African Americans in general. Yet what is imperative to note is the way in which she not only focuses on practical use of rhetorical device and sticks to simplicity in her speech but also crafts "practical" into an ideograph in the same ways she utilizes the imagery of being a citizen and being American.

RHETORICAL DEVICES USED IN MOSELEY BRAUN'S SPEECH

With the advent of media coverage in modern-day elections (and now with social media advertising) the modern presidential campaign announcement speech differs greatly from Chisholm to Moseley Braun to Harris. In the context of Moseley Braun's speech, there are several ways in which she considers her overall message, setting, audience, and value as a leader, not to mention the rhetorical situation in which she is presented. The optics (both favorable and unfavorable) offered by a live studio audience define and redefine audiences based not simply by distance but also by participation, specific news station, and commentary. Chisholm, as the first Black woman in Congress and as the first Black presidential candidate in general, garnered a great deal of attention and a generous following. Though Moseley Braun achieved many firsts of her own, as mentioned before, I contend the live televised speech did not work in her favor, in spite of the traditional and nontraditional rhetorical devices she used, social networking she confirmed from women's political groups and the historically Black college, and more.

In his 1970 article titled "The Effect of Television on Presidential Campaigns," Dan Hahn writes of the ways television serves as a help and hinderance for those running for the highest office in the land. He asks the question, "Does television automatically eliminate any potential candidate from the race?" By presenting this question, Hahn opens up a new way for scholars and society to think critically about nonverbal communication and audience perception. Because this article was two years shy of Chisholm's presidential announcement and well before the public political lives of Moseley Braun and Harris, I would assert his ideas did not even begin to consider the ways in which television could portray African Americans or women in general. However, he lists four considerations in his text regarding attractiveness, perceived wealth, public speaking ability, and position of prominence/celebrity.

In regard to all of these ideas, he suggests that television may underscore these things but does not immediately or affectively persuade audiences to choose a candidate solely based on them. However, in regard to Moseley Braun and her performance in a typically white space, even as she works to re-create space and redefine the presidency by existing within its considerations momentarily, scholars have pointed to several ways Black women are not regarded with the same respect and authority as their white female counterparts, among others, while on television. Karen Bowdre and Cory Brodnax remark about the ways in which the media portrays African American men and women through traditional stereotypes, particularly in television and film. Not only have they been portrayed as violent, criminals, and poor, but they state, "American culture African American women have been historically thought of in a way that justified their rape and mistreatment by those in the white majority" (2007, 15). Thus, when Moseley Braun repeats her claim of being practical three times, the phrase could have an oxymoronic effect on the typical C-SPAN audience. According to a March 2004 article penned by the Pew Research Center less than a year following Moseley Braun's announcement, the statistical data showed the majority of C-SPAN viewers were white at 70 percent rate, and 50 percent were women (Pew Research Center 2004). In the same study, only 15 percent were Black and most had a college education or college experience. Democrats and Independents made up the vast majority of the political identifications of their viewers at 37 percent and 30 percent, respectively (Pew Research Center 2004).

Thus, despite the fact Moseley Braun is dressed in a conservative Black dress suit, covering her knees and neck, has her hair pulled back in a neat bun, smiles at her audience and thanks her supportive (read white, liberal) women's groups, and swiftly opens with the rhetorical device zeugma, her speech automatically has no staying power because of the impractical position she exists within, history maker or not. The Oxford Dictionary (2020) defines zeugma as "a figure of speech in which a word applies to two others in different senses." An example of this occurs directly after she provides her greetings and salutations. She states, "I would like to thank all of the friends, supporters, and strangers, too, who have led me along my path toward this day" (Moseley Braun 2003, para. 4). By consciously thanking and considering her financial and political supporters, she not only demonstrates her command for public speech but also foreshadows the ability to do the work she discusses throughout her speech in "building bridges" and being steadfast in her presidential promises. Later, she uses a very vague but simple tricolon when she explains she wants to leave future Americans, like her niece Claire, "no less freedom, no less opportunity, no less optimism" as a virtue and value of the type of presidency she can bring. Yet she, of course, does not stop there.

As one of the most identifiable and easily inserted traditional rhetorical devices, Moseley Braun uses alliteration throughout her speech text. However, the way in which she does it should have cast an air of doubt in her listeners while comparing her perspective to the sitting president, or even some of her fellow Democratic contenders. Moseley Braun was the sole African American candidate in the 2004 presidential campaign, and although Clinton was a woman, it is already clear their political and social worlds were affected differently by this process. Thus, when Moseley Braun uses alliteration, she couples it with linking ideographs tied to American ideology, which could be her idea not only of practical persuasive techniques but also of how to position herself against the improbability of her candidacy.

For instance, the words "peace, prosperity, and progress" are not only used together but speak to her crowd regarding a historical American imperative and ideal that many try to achieve and even emigrate to the country in hopes of experiencing. Some of these key words build what many would regard to be part of the American Dream. Even though this phrase is metaphorical in nature and several people may respond to the idea differently, "poll data show that the Dream is more about spiritual happiness than material success for most Americans (although the percent stating 'material success' is on the increase)" (Hanson and Zogby 2010, 581). Although Hanson and Zogby's study was published approximately seven years after Moseley Braun's announcement speech, their findings are still germane to the ways in which a political candidate or general conversation, explicitly or implicitly, conceives of the American Dream.

What is more, the study also suggested:

> Poll data show that Americans associate political parties with the American Dream. Respondents were consistently more likely to say that the Democratic Party (in contrast to the Republican Party)

> will do a better job of helping more people achieve the American Dream, although the Republican Party has made some gains. Like others, we find consistency over time in attitudes about Blacks and minorities. Attitudes about the American Dream 581 that twice as many Americans blame Blacks for their own condition, as opposed to discrimination. The most recent data show a slight decrease in the trend showing agreement with this attitude. Although others have shown support for affirmative action to be consistently low, we find that a slight majority of Americans consistently support programs that make special efforts to help minorities get ahead in order to make up for past discrimination. (Hanson and Zogby 2010, 581)

Thus, while many Americans believe in helping others, the vast majority reject any association with the historical narrative of slavery and the depraved condition, rhetorical, political, economic, or otherwise laborious plight of African Americans specifically and minorities in general and their lack of control over racial discrimination. These conclusions to their numbers are not only alarming but truth-telling for a presidential persona that could be carried by a Black woman, no matter how well-spoken, dignified, pious, or practical she rehearses herself to become.

With this in mind, Moseley Braun's speech performance demonstrates her ability to adapt or be discursively adroit, which though it may be identified as a tactic of critical engagement, it is also practical, political, and particular to her situatedness as a Black woman running for office. She speaks to ideas of innovation, another American ideal, and personifies America with the traditional landmark of opportunity that, due to misuse and abuse of power, must "heal and renew" (Moseley Braun 2003, para. 9). Her idea of practical speaks to the metaphysical attributes of what an idealistic president should be and could be but is the opposite of what her body signifies in American society. She invites her audience to participate in the rebuilding of the ideals and innovation that has been broken, using "we" forty-five times within the course of her text and some variation of the word "build" seven times. Essentially, while some would argue Moseley Braun is working through using a feminist invitational rhetorical frame, I contend something else is happening in the midst of this, particularly taking into consideration the very constant backdrop of Black students, making her historic announcement at a historically Black institution of higher learning, and having her son lead her to the stage. These nonverbal gestures, in my perspective, speak louder than any words she says and demonstrate her hope to remain true to the institutions that are traditionally life giving for her, in spite of the impossible stage in which she is trying to win.

Movement 1: Smile as Practical Symbol, Symbols That Practically Sell

Throughout Moseley Braun's speech, her smile is almost infectious, bright, and wide, as if to pull her audience in through what may be first considered feminine style or even invitational rhetoric. Yet I contend neither of the two feminist perspectives are adequate to capture the social symbolism and cultural signifying a smile can communicate in an audience made up primarily of Black students and faculty at a historically Black institution with news media cameras at various angles. Wider, beaming smiles not only suggest intrinsic motivation (Cheng et al., 2019) but can also convey warmth while lacking a degree of position competence (Wang et al., 2017). Moseley Braun's smile speaks beyond her main audience and, I contend, attempts to sell the picture of a respectable mother of a loving son to everyone who may be listening in for the moment. As stated earlier, her first national position as senator was groundbreaking and remarkable, but that did not keep her safe from the subversive racist rules, regulations, roles, and procedures that can take place without a careful eye and ear around the chamber halls. And while in 1992 women's political role on the national scene copied Republican motherhood, Moseley Braun could no doubt factor in as such a role model then or in 2004. However, this supports the consideration that motherhood not only is biological but incorporates elements of performance (Oh 2009).

Introduced by her son, not only is Moseley Braun his biological mother, but as he is a college student at Howard, she has proven her worth, responsibility, and productivity in the social performance of Republican motherhood, but *in Black*. Michael Braun is not a statistic, nor is he a super predator functioning in the white hegemonic imagination as constructed by her (then) opponent Senator Clinton, but he is also articulate and demonstrates he is gaining social access on his own. To take this a step further, motherhood, in the case of Black womanhood, can be a politically and economically defined cultural contract. As Jackson (2002a) explains, "Cultural contracts can manifest themselves within and among persons, institutions, and cultures" (348).

If we take Jackson's theory further, we can apply it to political speech acts, particularly in regard to marginalized persons or those strategically cast outside of the norms of respectability, practicality, and political correctness. He explains:

> The cultural contracts paradigm suggests that at any given point in time human beings are coordinating relationships founded upon assimilation (ready-to-sign contract), adaptation (quasi-completed contract), or valuation of one another (cocreated contract). By

understanding what kind of contract(s) you have, as an African American communicologist, and determining when and why you signed it, it is possible to deconstruct your relational position in the academy and renegotiate your contract(s). The tragic reality is that most people do not understand the contracts they have signed much less the implications of having signed them. (Jackson 2002a, 362)

In all accounts, a smile may not immediately communicate radical subjectivity or display an ethic to re-create space or redefine a particular rhetorical persona, yet if we consider the ways in which smiles quite often articulate emotion, integrity, and sincerity, we would see this particular nonverbal persuasive device being used strategically within Moseley Braun's announcement speech. Not only do smiles sell, but they communicate a particular contractual agreement for political candidates, whether performing inside or outside of the gaze of heteronormativity. She uses a politics of practicality to sell her political persona not simply to those in the audience at Howard University but to those that would be watching the announcement on live television.

Yet due to Moseley Braun's use of a politics of practicality, she understands that she must, if possible and like Chisholm, negotiate on her own terms by choosing her announcer, audience, and even the people she acknowledges with her speech and the construction and performance of it. This is called the "cocreated cultural contract." Jackson continues to explain that they "are fully negotiable, with the only limits being personal preferences or requirements" (2002b, 48). However, her attempts, as history proves, are rejected, as she does not even make it to the Democratic primary. In this way, she is, indeed, displaying the tenet of radical subjectivity by rejecting the rules of normativity and trying to define her own.

Movement 2: The Next Best Thing

Carol Mosely Braun makes her announcement at what could be argued as the second most important institution in the Black community: the historically black college or university (HBCU). The majority of HBCUs were formed after Emancipation, not necessarily with a primary purpose to give Black students the same opportunity for educational attainment but to ensure further segregation from their white peers. During the 2011 Charles H. Thompson Lecture-Colloquium, Dr. M. Christopher Brown II delivered a paper titled "The Declining Significance of Historically Black Colleges and Universities: Relevance, Reputation, and Reality in Obamamerica," which was later published in *The Journal of Negro Education* (2013). Dr. Brown, president of

Alcorn State University, which was organized to accept, educate, and prepare Black students after Emancipation, considered the ways in which HBCUs are yet productive spaces of Black excellence but are feeling financial and enrollment pulls comparable to other universities. However, his study was charted after the presidency of Barack Obama, and it is not to say that the cultural relevancy of these bastions of higher learning is yet lost upon the community. It is a place where great leaders were able to shift their thinking in order to start movements. Within its walls lives one of the last hush harbors of the Black community, and as a sacred space, it serves people of African ancestry in ways predominantly white institutions can never imagine.

As a parent of a Howard student, Moseley Braun not only knows and understands the struggles and constraints of this space but, like Chisholm before her, most likely rationalized this setting would symbolize, more than a smile, who she was and what she stood for as a candidate. Particularly when considering a womanist analytical bend toward analyzing her speech, it is also imperative to understand the traditional ways in which she approaches her text and the unconventional means of doing so, as well. Like most presidential candidates, she opens with a salutation and greeting. Yet because the halls of the institution in which she stands are part of the historic Black community, her words mirror those of many traditional Black preachers, community leaders, and activists, as the individuals she thanks are welcoming her as their own, a member of the race, a member of the community but also, in her case, a parent of one of the students. Michael Braun had the privilege of introducing his mother to the community before she took the stage, and although his words were quick, his presence, not only as a Black male but as a student and member of the community, outlined her credibility and worth for taking part in sacred space.

Movement 3: "Let's Get This Young Lady Right Here. . . ."

In her book chapter titled "Mammies and Matriarchs: Feminine Style and Signifyin(g) in Carol Moseley Braun's 2003–2004 Campaign for the Presidency," Shanara Rose Reid-Brinkley writes, "All black women's performances of appropriate femininity are always already suspect within white supremacist discourse. In other words, black women must engage in a persistent, performative replication of propriety" (2012, 42). Because she is excluded from this category, and not included from the beginning, Moseley Braun's discursive space functions within a politics of practicality because she has to re-create, reconstruct, redefine, and reimagine space for herself. Even standing on the shoulders of Charlotta Bass and in particular Congresswoman

Shirley Chisholm, Moseley Braun is "fighting" like her predecessors and makes her case clear. Yet neither her voice nor her embodied discourse can quite grasp the impossible political stage that refuses to release her to do the work she feels compelled to do and qualified to achieve. With this being the case, we can easily overlook the ways in which she re-creates space for a womanist audience.

Rickey Hill (1994) defines the study of Black politics as "the purposeful activity of black people to acquire, use, and maintain power. The dimensions of Black politics are internal and external" (11). Hence, inclusion, in regard to Black women and the renegotiation of space, often does not happen. That is why efforts for their candidacy to move forward, even on the local level, is still hard to organize. Moving forward takes power, and even within the imperative of the communal will, Black political power is not as dominant a force based on historical and political constraints. Hill argues further, "They characterize a struggle for power, that is, the realization and defense of black people's objective interests and volition. This struggle for power reflects historical tensions and constraints between and among black people and white people. These tensions and constraints concerning optimum strategies for control and liberation, are grounded in the dominant-dominated relationship of the two groups" (11). The caricatures and challenges of American chattel slavery still perpetuate various stereotypes and struggles yet plaguing Black women today, and the fight for equality, equity, and inclusion has been a primary issue on several political platforms, particularly for Black women who stand within the intersections of tripartite oppression. So, when it comes to reconstituting the Black audience, and for all intents a womanist audience during the official beginning of a presidential campaign, some strategic and swift adjustments must be made by the rhetor.

One of the ways Moseley Braun controls her environment and crafts a womanist audience enmeshed in the tenet of traditional communalism is by choosing and defending her choice to choose one of the Black women students in the crowd. There is chatter before the young lady stands up to give her query to the candidate, quite possibly from the media. As posited earlier, the media has a specific agenda in place, and beyond purposely attacking the character and rhetorical record of Moseley Braun, their hope is to simply ask their questions first, with their viewers in mind. However, with a smile and quick pivot toward the student, she says, "Let's take this young lady first." In this moment, almost missed in the list of questions from the media that followed, Moseley Braun staunchly defines her campaign, even beyond the actual speech. Although the speech was read like a typical political candidate's words to the public, Moseley Braun's tone, mannerisms, and performance were tempered and tactful, much different than the tinge of excitement she begins to display when looking to the student.

In the section titled "The Gender Linkages" in Hanes Walton Jr.'s (1994) text *Black Politics and Black Political Behavior: A Linkage Analysis*, the culmination of tripartite oppression is finally explored. He writes, beyond the systemic and process forces and factors that are operating on the Black political experience, that one can find various individual-level ones. And among the individual-level ones is gender. The Black females, at least in Black life and politics, play a vital, creative, and dynamic role. Hence, it is postulated here that there is a relationship not only between gender and individual-level behavior but also between gender and other political units in the federal law system (207). Though anachronistic for Walton's text and Moseley Braun's candidacy, Bailey's (2018) understanding of misogynoir is still an excellent way to provide a foundation of contextualizing the immediate importance of Moseley Braun's creation, or at least her effort to create a safe Black political space for thought and exchange.

Movement 4: Coming to Voice Through a Politics of Practicality

For Black women to come to voice, a number of things must happen, including the creation of a space where she speaks and is seen as an individual worthy of speaking on her own behalf and where she can unleash the power for others to follow in her footsteps. When Moseley Braun discusses some of the "most noble ideals" of our country, she speaks to and beyond the crowd. Not only does she shift herself into the position of moral authority, much like she did against Helms, but she does this in a passive manner in which the crowd that understands the guise of counterlanguage, signifyin', and double consciousness understands how core her ideas are to their community, to those would-be advocates in the audience, and to the women's organizations that offered their support.

For the womanist rhetor to come to voice, she not only has to ignite her own intellectual curiosity and rhetorical wit to move beyond the unknown and the uninhabited space of a Black presidency but must invite others to do the same. By appealing to ideological constructs and metaphors that stand for the goodness of the country and the people that she has met, she pushes beyond portraying herself as a credible candidate by reaching out to the audience in front of her and beyond her. Moseley Braun's effort to make herself one of the many, as opposed to the only, Black woman contender for president demonstrated her understanding that the possibilities were slim for her to be seen as a possibility but to also be seen as a pious and responsible leader. Yet by working toward appealing beyond what may be seen to be the immediate audience, her efforts were not for mere optics but instead an effort to reimagine her voice in an accepting place that could uplift and encourage others to join into the conversation.

To consider herself to be "practical," to be introduced by her son on the campus of his historically Black university, and to think and comment it is *not* impossible to consider a Black woman as a worthwhile candidate for the American presidency is not only radically subjective behavior but rhetorically *impractical* and socially *impossible* and *improbable* by general stretches outside of the womanist prophetic imagination. Yet not by a stroke of genius but by a measure of effort and a hermeneutic of self-determination, Carol Moseley Braun charged forth to run for the Democratic nomination for the American presidency. Although she received little support, and had to leave the race before the party primary, her rhetorical persona, speech delivery, and actual text demonstrated the active discursive dismantling necessary on a political platform of such magnitude (Reid-Brinkley 2012, 35). The traditional tropes of Black womanhood and femininity and motherhood, as she politely smiles at her audience and confidently takes the stage to deliver her speech, were subdued and silenced by her tempered and tactful tone. Very little fire comes from her brow or breath, not to mention that her volume and voice do not shake with the same excitement of Chisholm. Nonetheless, she stands firmly behind the podium to deliver her words, no less empowered, no less undaunted by the goal of achievement before her.

In a 2010 interview with *The Root*'s Dayo Olopade, Moseley Braun shares some of her perspectives as a twenty-year veteran of state, local, and national politics, as well as her intuition for the future. As it relates to women, in general, she considers the ways in which women do not support women. Yet when centering her responses about Black womanhood and femininity, I contend she alludes to her loss, not her inability to be an effective leader, the efficacy of her speech text, or any other characteristic that did not exist in her political ability but the ability to win based on her womanish attitude. She explains: "Because black women have to work on being docile. There are some people who are naturally that way but I say what's on my mind, and I'm not going to *not* express my opinion or point of view because I'm the only girl in the room. I'm not built that way. Because I missed some of the cultural cues, particularly with regard to both gender and race, I was not as sensitive as I should have been. And I paid the price for it" (Olopade 2010). In this encumbered testimonial, there are far too many considerations to tease out in this space. However, as it pertains to the first movement in womanist rhetorical criticism, Moseley Braun understands that being a cocreator (Jackson 2002a) rejects possibilities of survival and thriving and is only made possible in a truly altruistic political space and egalitarian utopia that does not exist for Black women.

CONCLUSION

The daughter of a police officer and medical technician, Carol Elizabeth Moseley Braun was the first Black woman elected to the US Senate. She was only the second to arrange a viable candidacy for the presidency. Like Chisholm before her, Moseley Braun appeals to a womanist audience in some very innovative ways. Unlike Chisholm's fiery tone and quick-witted pace, possibly buttressed by the freedom to live a womanish lifestyle during some of her formative years while in Barbados, Moseley Braun's tone, temperament, and tendency toward public speech is polished, political, or, in her words, "practical." Her public persona is not only politically responsible but demonstrates her adaptability to her audience and the rhetorical situation and definite capability to address political and presidential matters with the hope to build bridges, as opposed to tearing them down and creating more work for others, typically those most marginalized by the intersectional existence of her own ontological positionality.

Before her historical announcement on September 22, 2003, given on the campus of Howard University in Washington, DC, only one other African American politician (male or female) had been publicly elected and successfully served as a US senator. That was Edward Brooke, who served from 1967 to 1979. However, the first African American to serve in the Senate was Hiram Rhodes Revels of Mississippi, serving from 1870 to 1871 to complete the term of Albert G. Brown. The second was Blanche Bruce, who also represented Mississippi from 1875 to 1881. Important to note is that both men served during the period of Reconstruction and were appointed by their states, not popularly elected like Brooke and Moseley Braun. However, while Moseley Braun was surrounded by other women colleagues in the Senate, her encounters with sexism were complicated by race. Beyond this, her contests surrounding issues of race were burdens left upon her shoulders alone, as there were no other Black senators during her tenure.

In conclusion, cocreation of the cultural contract "is often perceived as the optimal means of relational coordination across cultures, since the relationship is fully negotiable and open to differences. If a cultural contract is cocreated, there is an acknowledgment and valuation of cultural differences by all parties involved" (Jackson 2002b, 49). Like Zora Neale Hurston's character Janie from *Their Eyes Were Watching God*, Moseley Braun's wit, wisdom, and worth are dismissed in her efforts, and to a degree, she believes there is hope to spark a wave of change and ride the momentum for improving the reality of Black women everywhere, most notably her niece. Unfortunately, smiles did not get this done on the national stage.

Moseley Braun's rhetorical dismantling of dominant political rhetoric through a politics of practicality and a smile actively project a *womanist* sensibility and the same *in spite of* spirit garnered by Bass and Chisholm. Actively rejecting dominant discursive rules in order to garner some of the productive qualities of a symbol that can sell warmth as opposed to unfriendliness, cordiality and consciousness instead of lewd and licentious behavior, she offers another option to her audience with a cocreated cultural contract. Moseley Braun, throughout her career, made a conscious decision to smile wide and smile big when in various political arenas. She still does. Her smile, though filled with strategy, arguably dismantled the deafening air of defeat some would have her carry before she could even begin her speech, rebuttal, or challenge. I argue that she created her own contract (and her smile was a brick and blueprint) and hoped her contemporaries would cosign. This was not simply done within the presidential announcement speech but everywhere she knew her voice and ability would be challenged. These were spaces not intended for her to speak but she poised herself to take them on, nonetheless. However, the price for coming alive by processing through the womanist tenets within the safety of community, compassion, and care and thereby rejecting society's pull can be high. She did not win the race but quite possibly afforded space for others to follow. Arguably, Harris caught the fire to ignite her own dream of the Senate and eventually her own race for the presidency.

Chapter 5

"Dreamers Cannot Afford to Sit Around"

The Presidential Campaign Announcement Speech of Senator Kamala Devi Harris

> The fight of Black women has always been fueled and grounded in faith and in the belief in what is possible, we have always built the future that we can see, and believe in, and fight for. It's why Sojourner spoke. It's why Mae flew. It's why Rosa and Claudette sat. It's why Maya wrote. It's why Fannie organized. It's why Shirley ran. And why I stand here as a candidate for president of the United States.
> —SENATOR KAMALA HARRIS

In 2019, Senator Kamala Harris attended the Essence Festival in New Orleans, Louisiana, following in the candidate pathways of former president Barack Obama and former secretary of state Hillary Clinton. As one of the largest Black cultural meccas in the United States, New Orleans not only is a historical landmark composed of intercultural and cross-cultural influences but is also distinctively impacted by rich African diasporic retentions interspersed within its language, cuisine, music, and everyday life. Harris gave the statement above before an audience primarily made up of Black women, who, for almost thirty years, have brought a vast array of issues to the fore of this particular festival. The issues, which have included more than romantic relationships and spirituality, bring conversations centering health, economic empowerment, sisterhood, and activism. This "party with a purpose," as it is often called, has served as a bastion for cultural creativity, artistic expression, and social preservation. Since 1995 the Essence Festival, coordinated at the end of the New Orleans Jazz & Heritage Festival by the magazine of the same name, has highlighted several legends, including African American civil rights activists Al Sharpton and Jesse Jackson, demonstrating not only the faith-based leanings of participants but the profound parallel of political philosophy as part and parcel to daily Black life as well (Fensterstock 2016). With this in mind, it is quite possible Harris's rhetorical resonance among attendees sparked the collective memory and ongoing experience of tripartite oppression through considering historically significant figures, whose faith and politics coalesced in public and private spaces of discourse.

Standing on the shoulders of the giants she invoked, I would argue that for the 500,000 attendees, of which 90 percent were African American women, Harris's presence spoke well into and beyond this historical legacy, not simply as a Black candidate but as a Black woman (Fensterstock 2016). Studies demonstrate that Black voters in general consider political homogeneity and ideological congruity as one of the primary factors when supporting a candidate for public office. Although they do not vote only based on the likeness of social experience, it is also more likely that Black voters will vote for Black women in comparison to white women and white men (Lerman and Sadin 2016). This is imperative to note, not only for the impending analysis of Harris's speech. It also governs the way in which certain audiences see or do not see Black women as viable leaders for office or, more importantly, representative of who epitomizes their values. When a Black woman presents herself as a contender for president of the United States, the Black community listens intently. They shift and sift through the pandering publics to form and frame a separate audience to support a common cause, whether they eventually have the chance to vote for the Black woman speaking or not. Within this space to be formed, the typical rhetor seeks to moderate a message that will buttress social equality and an opportunity for the marginalized to be heard. Yet in the moments surrounding Harris's official announcement in Oakland and the public appearances to follow, securing the Black vote or Black women's support was not the true challenge of her campaign. Instead, it was carefully weaving together a powerful narrative that would rightly divide words of truth *for the people*. Her audience was designed beyond those physically assembled and defined in spite of the strictures of her predecessors, Chisholm and Moseley Braun.

At what could be argued to be a theoretical crossroads between intersectionality, Black feminism, and womanist rhetorical theory lies the narrative style of then Senator Kamala Harris. Before her words and position could lean toward what seems to be an Afrofuturist recalibration for political possibilities unknown, her presence as a candidate was met with excitement and energy. Her speech, full of inclusive statements and truth-telling moments, exists in a multicultural, multinational, and multilingual space as its backdrop. Amid the chant of "Ka-ma-la," the people did not hesitate to show their support, admiration, and sheer inquisitive nature to be a part of this historic event of her official announcement. This is a public space about to be reimagined. It was and is a structure that stands as a symbol of freedom for some, while for others a dungeon of despair, despondency, and detention (C-SPAN 2019). Still, ruminating beyond this dichotomous discursive display of realities, Oakland City Hall was reclaimed as something else for Harris and *the people* providing her room to come to voice as their candidate. In these moments that are hers, I contend Harris attempts to bring together the legacy and prophetic prowess of Chisholm into conversation with the politics of practicality that anchored Moseley Braun.

In her effort to re-create a new reality and redefine the electability and reality of a Black woman as a viable candidate for president of the United States of America, I argue Senator Harris hopes to transcend the letdowns of the past and the frustrations of the present and to propose herself as the face for the future. Thus, in this chapter, I continue to work through quilting together womanist methods and modes from literary theory, political communication, and Afrofuturism to determine how Harris's speech conceives a new, organic approach. As we historically have considered Black women in politics, we have yet to witness their rise to be second-in-command. However, our current reality has been changed and in the years to come, Harris's announcement speech and those to follow will be considered in a new manner. In order to glean what Harris does through this final application of womanist rhetorical criticism, I will again provide a biosketch of Harris. This will allow readers and hearers to consider how her cultural identity shaped her intellectual musings and political discourse. After this, I will ponder the ways in which Sankofa and Afrofuturist womanist discourse can be applied to the way in which she ultimately reimagines conventional spaces beyond their currently perceived limits. By charting them as alternative spaces to reconceive present-day norms for those within the mire of the margins, she is not only formidably calling for change but in many ways forcing the narrative to accept it.

CONTEXTUALIZATION

The prophetic gaze of Chisholm that situates itself directly in the pulpit of the traditional jeremiad of many historical African American politicians, preachers, and social prophets alike has set the tone for many presidential announcement speeches. Former president Barack Obama and secretary of state Hillary Clinton both looked to her candidacy and congressional service as a rubric to design their own sights toward the Oval Office. Moseley Braun added her own brand of political precarity and ingenuity by unleashing a politics of practicality in an effort to undercut the Bush II administration. Then, years later, Harris found herself on a public stage in front of thousands of people. At that time, she was able to pick from two contests of Black women from her political party. The immediate red thread she ties between her candidacy and the two other Black women who have previously run begins with culture and true civility. Her reference to the work ethic of her mother speaks to the culturally specific ways in which family relationships are important to maintain. The second note she makes is to the fierce social strivings her parents sought through their immigration to the United States and activity in the civil rights movement.

True civility, in my summation, includes any effort to take up the charge of the late congressman John Lewis: "Get in good trouble." Whether on purpose or not, trouble is already in the air and she embarks as another challenger to the incumbent, President Donald J. Trump. With a clearly diverse crowd backing her, this immediate picture of diversity builds a narrative criticism of the then current commander in chief. By sheer visual representation during the broadcasts internationally streaming her speech, with little or great effort Harris crafts a constructive ploy toward building an ideological critique of what America is and what it should be as well as hope for what it can become under her leadership. Who, then, can truly prove themselves to be truly American, then, by the first snapshots of the crowd produced by Harris, other than her? Speaking to the love and appreciation for her country but especially the people of Oakland, she narrates her own story at the opening of her speech.

With a traditional opening, Harris offers thanks to the mayor of Oakland, while exclaiming that her heart is full where she stands. These are necessary and critical opening gestures toward feminist invitational rhetoric but are still situated in the protocol of most political speech making. However, as a native of California, this is not borrowed space and is instead a familiar place for her to be. Posturing herself carefully and squarely in the seat of being a "proud daughter of Oakland" by explaining not only the "longstanding friendship" she and Mayor Libby Shaft have shared but that their mothers were also friends. After explaining, "I was born just up the road at Kaiser Hospital," the crowd she is appealing to immediately responds with cheers of praise. It is here that we can gain immediate evidence that Harris's rhetorical posturing may not necessarily be womanist or tightly wound up in a Black feminist perspective, but indeed its methodological scope offers something that critically contrasts the norm. Indeed, she borrows from what Foss and Griffin deem invitational rhetoric but adds more to its typical characterization.

One of the primary goals of Foss and Griffin's (1995) invitational rhetoric is to dismantle the intrigue of persuasion. They argue that rhetoric, with its bend toward persuasion, "has been defined as the conscious intent to change others" (Foss and Griffin 1995, 2). Thus, for Harris to purposefully invite such diversity into her platform demonstrates her willingness to hear and see others but automatically criticizes her primary opponent, and his inability to do the same. Wells et al. (2020) consider the ways in which President Trump utilizes the broadcast reach of social media beyond traditional news sources to establish what they call an attentive public or one that allocates its attention to particular objects, ideas, or in this case texts *and tweets*. While this is the opposite job of Harris's overall campaign, and certainly within her speech, what is clear is that her efforts to draw her crowd into her ideas, not simply as traditional spectators. She uses a method that invites the public to participate and cocreate. Still, her inherently intersectional approach positions her differently than a woman without a racialized experience. Amid the Black faces in a traditionally white space, those within her audience respond to her vocal gestures as a story similar to their own.

Born to two immigrant parent-scholars who met as activists in the civil rights movement, Kamala Devi Harris has shared her "stroller-eye view" of seeking justice for those who needed it most. Her mother (Shyamala), an endocrinologist, and her father (Donald), an economist, though divorcing during her elementary years, encouraged intellectual growth, fairness, and a strong cultural identity for their daughters. This upbringing to invite a hearing ear and a warm embrace to inclusion, equity, and equality through social justice not only is clear throughout her announcement speech but is underscored in the way in which she speaks of her family's influence in her upbringing and vision of the world, particularly considering that her mother, while not a Black woman, is still South Asian, an immigrant, and Hindu.

Although her parents were immigrants, one Black and the other a woman of color, Harris's pedigree speaks to the longstanding myth that

Black women do not have the educational attainment behind their name to achieve feats of great attainment. As she explains in her opening remarks, her parents were students at the University of California–Berkley, which is considered to be one of the more prestigious public universities, and the crowd seemed all too familiar. Instead of building a connection with her own experiences at a historically Black university, she reins in on her association with the state that voted for her to represent their interests in the Senate and, quite possibly, leans on the details of locale. This crowd, filled with noticeable representatives of the Black community, possibly does not need a reference to an institution in which she has direct experience; it could either demonstrate her pull toward the ideal Californian vision to dream or serve as a strategic maneuver to extend beyond a very tight and specific link that the majority of the polis would neither have nor desire to acquire. Still, its mention could detract from the redefining of space she is using this speech moment to chart. As this Oakland space and community are being rebranded in her political vision, not as a sports town or as a bed of crime, her rhetorical persona invites new possibilities but not necessarily a decidedly feminist style. Whereas a utopia may not necessarily be a fitting word, the seeds she is scattering are watered with womanist visions of thriving, even if we cannot altogether dismantle the building itself.

By inviting her audience to be a part of the speech, instead of listening patiently until she is finished, it is immediately clear that Harris's intention is broader than can be held in a building or a campus. This announcement speech presents her dedication to a multicultural and multilingual vision of the future. Her training as a lawyer and the lead attorney of the state of California postures her rhetoric in spaces where her message can take on multiple meanings for multiple people. The amount of time she takes to stylistically posture herself to this audience breaks apart from a traditional womanist or Black feminist analytical vision at certain moments. However, the purposeful political future she sees beyond the speech event adds to a dimension of inquiry within womanist theory: reciprocity and partnership.

Over the years, there has been a great debate between who can claim the womanist moniker. Although I explore this topic briefly in chapters 1 and 2, within the discipline of communication, this matter has not been as commonly discussed, nor have the rules been clearly defined with a sizable example. Harris, like her Black woman counterparts on the campaign trail to the White House, does not suggest she ascribes to a Black feminist, womanist, or otherwise decisive ideological standpoint. Her lack of choosing may not only be political but is certainly due to accessibility of a spectrum of choices that well fit her circumstances.

The content and context of her speech do not immediately offer any specific mark of theoretical delineation. Yet the pretext in which she exists within might—in this world of folding chairs—situate *her* rhetorical persona as the necessary accessory to bring to meetings where seats were refused, at the ready for a brawl with white supremacists. Her presence alone builds a nation, while her absence can shatter a world. Either way, moving in and out and beyond rhetorical space, Harris makes the decision to allow herself the privilege to choose how she dares to be herself within the moment. She pushes the envelope of what was once damned and diminished Black voice by using three distinct moments to jettison her announcement on the campaign trail: at Essence, at the beginning of *Good Morning America* on Martin Luther King Jr. Day, and finally in front of Oakland City Hall. By making herself a clear contender through what, at times, seems to be the makings of even an Afrofuturist womanist expanse for a Black woman's political possibilities in a very possible reality, her imminent witness still chooses to stand within her reality between two identities.

To the trained eye, she does not staunchly stand within the vision of Sankofa, as her vision of the future is only loosely constructed with a traditional womanist and Black feminist vision. Arguing, analyzing, and theorizing the direction of Harris's immediate intentions within any brand of Afrocentric or decidedly marginalized theoretical strategy is not particularly evident on the surface. Notwithstanding, the moments in between her pauses, the combination of the audience and the broad grasp of the polis, and still the obvious excitement of the day does not preclude or exclude the facts: she stands upon the shoulders of Chisholm and Moseley Braun. She has also lived in a world that has experienced the two-term presidency of Barack Obama and the racist vitriol and political outrage that created political, economic, and social instability for so many.

Sankofa, which in the Adinkra language loosely means "to go back and fetch it" or to retrieve something that was lost/taken, is produced rhetorically by the rhetor reconstructing discursive space through reclaiming personhood, dignity, and honor, if we are to think through Atwater (2009). However, beyond her mother, Harris instead finds herself standing in the merit of a newfound method for politicians that only her white counterparts can grasp, achieve, and maintain. To some degree, none of this matters. Otherwise, every bit of it does. Nonetheless, I stand to contend that the rhetorical rub of Harris's campaign announcement speech stands somewhere in between. The conditions of the day, which include the political reality and rhetorical geography of the time call for her response to *do something* different. What Harris comes up with on the dais certainly breaks into a new mold for society to chart, and this chapter works to explore that.

MAKING THE INVISIBLE VISIBLE:
CRAFTING WOMANIST UTOPIAS IN DYSTOPIAN TIMES

Since 2000, the number of Black women serving in elected positions that extend to the national level has dramatically increased. At this time, very little peer-reviewed scholarship is available to contextualize the life and career of Vice-President Harris. This is quite possibly the first extensive text that considers her political rhetoric despite the fact she is only the second woman of color, let alone African descent, to serve as a US senator and now the first as vice president of the United States. Although her speech does not make up for all of the deep considerations we, as scholars, should take up to study her politics, personhood, and beyond, the fact that her presidential campaign speech situates itself as only the third in its national reach to embody and use the rhetorical strategies available to a Black woman is still something very new and unique. Her speech is in a league of its own. To this end, her rhetoric, political platform, presidential candidacy, and overall career deserves intense research and consideration. Pushing beyond this generalist view, I suggest her speech opens the door for conversations surrounding an Afrofuturist political vision in real time, taking into consideration Black feminist and womanist visions for dignity, personhood, and merit on the political stage. While "Afrofuturism has always been concerned with creatively telling the histories of those from the African diaspora while also designing new narratives," (Gipson 2019, 85) I believe that an Afrofuturist womanist political vision designs a narrative with a Black woman as the rhetorical starting point but also as the active agent in shifting the sociopolitical paradigm. Yet this begs to pose the question of whether or not we are charting Black women's speech with the correct measure. Certainly, there *must* exist potential in re-creating a world where there is more than enough space to carry forth a future where a Black woman is president. Is this only available within the days of a future that has passed us by in our creative rhetorical imaginary? Is there a specific rhetorical hermeneutic of eschatological strivings that we should utilize? Or is our current plane the best we have?

This line of questing is offered not to diminish the Black women who have worked tirelessly to come to voice and hold political office at the highest levels. It is instead offered in an effort to challenge the ways anti-Blackness and misogynoir have denied our ability to envision *a whole new world*. Despite the fact that Black women are consistently moving into more powerful political roles, their constituents widely reflect either their own ontological experience in this world or, in the least, match their political ideology. In "#BlackGirlMagic Demystified: Black Women as Voters, Partisans and Political Actors," Gillespie and Brown (2019) contend, "Black women often face significant challenges to securing political representation and advocates who will champion their issues" (49). They further explain that according to the Center for American Women and Politics, there are seven Black women who serve as mayors of the 100 largest cities in America, and "of the 2,131 women state legislators, 312 are Black. These electoral gains happened in a point in time where Black women's median wages were $36,735 per year compared to the median wages of $60,388 annually for White men" (Gillespie and Brown 2019, 49).

As Harris exclaimed in her speech, Black women make only sixty cents to every white man's dollar, making their real earning power 40 percent less than that of the privileged standard-bearer. And because Harris makes this point squarely dealing with race and gender, the reclamation of space and place for Black women and the communities that support them becomes an important issue to consider for her platform, whether passively or directly.

Whether we look back at historical accounts such as Harriet Jacobs's *Narrative of the Life of a Slave Girl*, the quest for Belinda's recompense in the late eighteenth century, or even the way in which Phillis Wheatley's voice and genius is placed on trial for the audacity to pen such prolific and profound poetry, Black women have been denied their say. In Daina Berry's text *The Price for Their Pound of Flesh: The Value of the Enslaved, from Womb to Grave, in the Building of a Nation* (2017), she does not simply discuss the price of the enslaved African from the cradle to the grave in the context of American chattel slavery but also describes the ways in which Black women and men were dehumanized and any potential for citizenship cast away. Of course, this was all made sanctified by justification through Scripture and stamped by the letter of the law. Never were Black women (or the men they loved) meant to be writers, poets, entrepreneurs, or presidents. Neither were they to be considered *presidential*. Thus, if Harris's speech can exist within a space to push the envelope and challenge the rules of hegemonic whiteness, a shift can be made toward such an Afrofuturistic political plane located somewhere in Wakanda, building from the Afrocentric ethic of Sankofa but not limited by the imagination of Haile Gerima, Stan Lee (with later help from Ryan Coogler), or even Julie Dash. Yet an Afrofuturist vision welcoming justice, order, peace, and balance within a political world order seemingly approaching anarchy or at least lacking rhetorical prestige within the presidency is something Harris's speech welcomes passively by situating itself within such an audience and in front of such a backdrop.

The first academic text created to situate Afrofuturism as a larger aesthetic mode was *Flame Wars: The Discourse of Cyberculture* by Mark Dery (1994). This book studied a diverse range of artists working in different genres and media who were united by their shared interest in projecting black futures derived from Afrodiasporic experiences (Yaszek 2006, 48). Dery's work against a set definition makes the availability to shift and to shape an Afrofuturist political vision, or at least make it available. Granted, Harris may not consider this to be the means or modes of her method toward crafting her message. However, the strivings are similar, if not wholly the same because one of the most important characteristics of Afrofuturism is the use of Sankofa. Her broader speech focuses on the act of looking back toward understanding the past in order to understand the future as a first step. More importantly, she crafts and delivers her speech in a way that wields a new return, not an old one. Christel Temple (2010) explains that in the United States and other diasporan communities, Sankofa has an informal legacy as related to ideologies of "return" or "back to Africa"; however, modern waves of African migration and travel, particularly of Akan/Ghanaian representatives as well as diasporan Africans who have traveled to Ghana and accumulated liberating traditional African cultural references, have placed cultural informants in the diasporan midst. These cultural informants have been able to provide more accurate descriptions of the conceptual roots and uses of Sankofa in the United States (Temple 2010).

Although Temple lists symbolic demonstrations of going back to African cosmologic influence of being due to the disruption of the *Maafa*, or the African slave trade, she does not explicitly make the case for this definition to be used in a strictly communication context. However, to stretch her definition for Harris's efforts, I contend the speech's energies work toward reclaiming and reconstituting a political space that was denied African ancestors upon their kidnap, rape, and capture but also in pushing forth the dreams of those that dared to believe beyond the violent past of the country and look toward its possibilities.

Following this, realizing the freedom to "dream" or be a dreamer, much like her parents and many of her audience members, allows her to craft a new vision between the space of technological advancement and radical transformation, all without forcing stand-in bodies for the always and already colonized. However, many of these methods are not altogether womanist, and the way in which Harris attempts to stand in the confidence of the space she has created still speaks broadly to womanist sentiments, if we widen our aperture.

Layli Phillips offers in her introduction to *The Womanist Reader: The First Quarter Century of Womanist Thought* (2006) the idea that womanism is a social change perspective rooted in Black women's and other women of color's everyday experiences and everyday methods of problem solving in everyday spaces, extended to the problem of ending all forms of oppression for all people, restoring the balance between people and the environment/nature, and reconciling human life with the spiritual dimension (xxi). She adds, "Womanist methods of social transformation cohere around the activities of harmonizing and coordinating, balancing, and healing. These methods work in and through relationship, reject violence and aggression but not assertiveness, and readily incorporate 'everyday' activities. These overlapping methods include but are not limited to, dialogue, arbitration and mediation, spiritual activities, hospitality, mutual aid and self-help, and 'mothering'" (Phillips, xxvii). Charting Phillips's considerations, the foundation of womanism as a social theory simply seeks to deconstruct white hegemonic patriarchal forces against marginalized bodies utilizing all means of persuasion available. Thus, any rhetor looking to achieve a new vision of the world through solidarity, self-determination, and an ethic of spiritual, physical, and mental wholeness may not be able to count themselves as *womanish* in their efforts but can reciprocate *in kind*. After all, womanist, Black feminist, feminist, and other marginalized ideological standpoints see reciprocity, partnership, and action as a means of crafting a better political experience for all.

TRADITIONAL CRITICISM

In many ways, Harris's speech rejects all forms of traditional rhetorical criticism, outside of the assorted ideological critiques she weaves throughout her arguments. From a womanist analytical read, her usage of anaphora, alliteration, and other rhetorical devices, used in comparison to Chisholm and Moseley Braun, are different but not deficient. The outcome of Harris's use leans her appeals toward pathos so that her readers may identify with her. Arguably, she wants to be seen as an individual but still a part of a larger, more important community geared toward a *dream*. She does not necessarily want to be seen solely as a prosecutor, or even as a presidential candidate, but as one who dares to accentuate the possibilities of the universal dream we all have: equality. While the *American Dream* is an ideograph unto itself, still Harris frames her perspective of a dream as one that is still to come. I call this the Afrofuturistic political possibility framed in "the not yet." It is best understood in the eschatological divine of many religions but it is still held within the realness of her hope for this dream of *the people* to be realized for all people. Notably, this heavy lean toward pathos and potentially away from constructing herself as an effective, credible candidate demonstrates her rejecting the need to prove herself in the same way Chisholm and Moseley Braun worked so hard to maintain within their speech delivery.

On the surface, there is something that seems very Burkean in this discursive move, and even calls back to the efforts of Obama and Clinton, who pivot toward the American Dream and feminist style. Instead, I assert that invoking a call to shared emotion, empathy, and identification with her listeners, what seems like a politician's pedantic pandering upon the platform, is an effort to do something the other Black women before her were not permitted to experience. Quite possibly, Harris's reality following two Black women as candidates and that of President Obama offers a level of purpose to push beyond what may be critically relevant to Black women's experience but instead push toward the totality of a womanist vision of thriving. It seems as though Harris is rejecting a baseline of exploring embodied discourse and accepting an effort to instead build toward intersectional identification. Yet there still remains the constant reminder of space and place, refusing to afford her the full breadth of normative exposure and experience. While her speech may not be decidedly womanist in its classification, there are still elements of her approach to break the mold that make a bold case that she is hoping to draft something beyond her situatedness as a Black woman.

Beyond intersectionality and inclusive language, Harris situates herself as the candidate who wants to take on the responsibility for shifting the country into a better position. By listing out the ways in which the ideological landscape of the "America" our parents dreamed to experience is *not* the America we are experiencing today, she deems the old vision of America the problem. It is the one that is in moral crisis. It is the one that needs to prove its ethical worth, not her. She says: "We are here because we have another battle ahead. We are here knowing that we are at an inflection point in the history of our world. We are at an inflection point in the history of our nation. We are here because the American Dream and our American democracy are under attack and on the line like never before. We are here at this moment in time because we must answer a fundamental question" (Harris 2019).

By identifying a new problem and taking the burden of proof off the back of Black women, she subverts what originally looks to be a feminist style point and offers up something different. Without using the traditional tools for others to notice, she repositions her speech as a jeremiad. Black women are not the problem; therefore, they need not defend their candidacy. Immigrants are not the root of systemic injustice and built the columns that stand behind her, so they should be able to stand before it proudly. By subjecting America to an ethical and ideological makeover project, she admits that there is a great deal of work to do but undermines the patriarchal devices before her. This is not the sort of invitation the crowd expects, and it does not follow what some of the public surrounding her sorely believes it needs.

She later says, "Lord knows I'm not perfect," almost giving an account or apology for her own situatedness in the massive mania that exists at the time of her speech but the corrective she offers brushes into the space, not of cunning but of subversion. This is the space I would argue is *beyond* normative persuasion. On the surface, she is overemphasizing her identifying factors with the audience and projects herself away from the dream of King and beyond the visions of Chisholm and Mosley Braun. She portrays herself outside of the dreaming of her parents. She is even further beyond the dream of the ancestors she tries to invoke in front of a city hall that represents so many other city halls across the country. These are the same spaces that refused justice to a certain people. Formerly, her use of pathos seemed to display a sharp move away from what should be seen in a Black woman's presidential announcement speech. Yet I am convinced, again, that she is not simply reclaiming the time never fully returned to Congresswoman Maxine Waters but reconstructing space for *all of us* to not simply be viewed but to be seen and heard.

Movement 1: The Truth Shall Set You Free or Tell the Truth and Shame the . . .

Not only does the Afrocentric divine tenor of "the truth shall set you free" point us back to religious language found in many faith traditions, the call to "tell the truth and shame the devil" speaks to the same moral consciousness Harris tries to call for in her speech. In particular, this African American cultural aphorism considers the need to expose the ineffectiveness and immorality of normative culture. It does not take only an ethical mandate but a passion to do the right thing, call for the right thing, and know how to do it while everyone is looking. The popular adage of Western society would say that the emperor has no clothes. Within a Black cultural context, this statement signifies that when something is wrong there is a deep, convicting moral call to make it right. Yet even by the time Harris discursively desires to right old wrongs, she has difficulty reaching beyond the crowd before her speech and into the public beyond it. While her audience is welcoming and affords her the agentive voice she desires, the road toward a national political journey realistically does not kindly welcome her into their homes, heads, and hearts.

According to US Census data used for an essay drafted by the American Association of University Women, Black women in the United States earn only sixty-eight cents to every dollar earned by white men (Nelson 2018). Thus, "the wealth gap can help us to understand why black women's earnings are so far behind those of both white men *and* white women. In 2013 the median white household had 13 times the wealth ("wealth" refers to total assets minus debts) of the median black household—specifically, the median white household had about $134,000 to the median black household's $11,000" (para. 5). Such brash statistics of our country's economic situation do not fare well for the least of these: those marginalized on the furthest side of society.

Harris makes a singular specific statement toward affirming Black women. In some ways it is *enuf.* As it speaks to the *truth of the matter* and takes up these statistically relevant factors head on and without a quiver in her oral presentation, her call for feeling a communal pull to make America live up to its ideals is a difficult rallying cry to force. Here, Harris's move toward radical subjectivity in rejecting the norm that is before us does not fully reimagine or redefine this portion of structural oppression. The plan to implement economic justice is one that many candidates rally around but very few are able to see put into action. Moreover, whereas Harris's speech functions as an imperfect model for traditional womanist thought, it is simultaneously working toward new visions of womanist possibilities. The legacy of economic injustice, again, is not the sole cause in which she is fighting to correct but it is one that undermines Black women's ability to rise to the prominence of the typical narratives we must highlight as canonically relevant, right, and those we must cite. In this vein, considering the text of the speech, Harris's words allow us to see that a womanist rhetorical theory or a womanist rhetorical criticism forces the rhetor to investigate beyond what is typically considered sensible and fair. It also necessitates our understanding of the very nature of Black women's embodied discourse beyond reclaiming ethos but into forging conversations about what Black women *feel* and how others must see it as their duty to respond in kind. As her body and voice show up, on one accord, together, not separate, one from others, we see that Harris's speech provides a model for us to see something different and for us to live into a reality we have always desired.

To explain, Jacqueline Jones Royster (2003) says, "Western rhetorics, at least the legacies of them that we have inherited through scholarship, are demonstrably dominated by elite male viewpoints and experiences" (149). I take this to mean and suggest for the arguments of this manuscript that normative theories of communication are discourses disinterested in the particular. They are those that readily race to oversimplify and run to fault the essentializing of experience. With Harris's speech as an example, I bravely take the leap to say that this is held within a fear that they may no longer be human due to their incapacity to truly feel. As the overarching goal of identification among audience members is met, and the rhetor from the normative public can move beyond the scope of the statement that struck a chord with the polis, he (or she) shrouded in whiteness becomes, once again, disembodied but still capable of being destroyed. Royster maintains that contemporary scholars who seek to shift these viewpoints and paradigms, to extend the boundaries of interest and inquiry, or to reendow these spaces with the materiality of other lives face an abiding challenge. We are called upon to create conditions that have the capacity to enable scholars in the area to even imagine the rationality of standing in other places, or inquiring with contrasting interests, or paying attention to different sets of features that may not currently be within the scope of credibility. In other words, disciplinary practices have built up a high intolerance to the assigning of value and credibility to any site, focal point, theory, or practice other than those whose contours are already sanctioned historically within the circle of understanding (150).

For the case of Harris, or another Black woman political candidate, this means the framing of their rhetorical musings must match up with the tenacity of Mrs. Sohpia's "Hell no" from *The Color Purple* and the confidence of *Black Panther*'s Okoye in response to reframing the linguistic and liminal simpleness of CIA agent Eric Ross *before* he experiences Wakanda. When Ross ponders upon the General's ability to speak English by ignoring her and only placating to T'Challa because of his royal stance, he is met with her ability to not only be radically subjective in rejecting rigid notions of rhetorical fluidity but also a thought process that moves beyond the cognitive dissonance they are all trying to process in their current situation. When Okoye responds, "when she wants to" as Ross inquires, her sly smile and a quick-witted response does not overstep her bounds behind her king but employs the redemptive dance that must flow within the womanist rhetors embodied voice, presence, and standards that an audience among her must respect (Coogler 2018). Similarly, Mrs. Sohpia denies Miss Millie the gratification of petting her children and willfully becoming her maid. Although what happened after these responses sent their worlds into spirals, the audacity to *feel* their truth and stand (ten toes down) within it is made of the same substance as Harris's projection of blame and refusal of shame.

Movement 2: K.A.M.A.L.A. as a Site of Rhetorical Spectacle

At the beginning of this deep dive into Harris's announcement speech, I framed the space in which her highlighted quote at the top of the chapter was given. These words were shared at a site and place that sits firmly between urban spectacle, cultural preservation, and communicative exchange. At its heart, Gotham explains, "Tourism stands at the nexus of global forces of transnational flows and networks of activity, and local forces of territorial embeddedness and place particularity" (2007, 226). I would argue that places of public memory that become artifact function similarly. However, for the concerns of this study, the spectacle is not simply the site or place in which the narrative of the speech is created but its immediacy with the rhetor and the performance of the day is what matters most.

In Frantz Fanon's *Black Skin, White Masks* ([1952] 2008), he is famously quoted as saying, "I cannot go to a film without seeing myself. I wait for me. In the interval, just before the film starts, I wait for me. The people in the theater are watching me, examining me, waiting for me." In a similar way, the crowd waits for Kamala, not the senator or the former attorney general of the state of California but the woman whose name, like Barack Obama's, sounds quite different than the rest of the field. Yet Kamala does not immediately appear. In spite of the American Sign Language interpreter just below her, only seen at the first point of her entry on the stage, would-be womanist audience members wait for Kamala Devi Harris to reposition herself as a candidate on the political stage. While we think we are familiar with this stage and yearning to move into futures that have our voices and considerations in mind, we wait to see what happens next amid the nervous cheering.

In this version of the future, we move beyond the fantastic, exceed the vision of spectacle, not to be waited upon to be impressed in the same way exhibitionists urge for performative gratification of the white polis. We, as audience members ready to provide agentive voice and protection no matter what, exist wholly within and outside and beyond the intersectional spaces of Black femininity, womanhood, motherhood, and even an Afrofuturist political possibility. Once again, this reclamation of space and place through the backdrop of the government building must not be upheld, or at least envisioned as entirely salvageable at first glance. It must instead be rhetorically reconstructed with the same bricks Wanda Coleman's womanish wiliness advises. In this brief sonnet of embodiment, there lies the need to restructure credibility, the desire to feel, and the call for shaping a vision of a womanist rhetorical present and future.

Black women's bodies disembodied and disassembled beyond the spectacle of colonial infantilization as articulated by Fanon is an ongoing political experience. It is often placed on public display with very little to exchange outside of making promiscuous the pride of her productivity outside of (and even within) the polis. In ways that intersect with the differently abled and hearing-impaired audience searching and seeking for the interpreter to communicate well the same hopes and strivings the hearing crowd can experience, Black women's bodies search and seek. They seek for space to be repaired and reconstructed by their own visions of the future and a present that cannot simply be tolerated. It is a culture that wills the promotion of healing. It is the emotional space available to thrive *in spite of*. In the spectacle that remains of the place of the speech, the dis-abled, disassembled body remains rhetorically powerless and yet fixated on the facts of heteronormative discursive rank and file, as is the chart for the day: a space that would push the margins of thought to dance dynamically beyond sheer rejection and toward deep contemplation for tangible taskings toward thriving. Harris does not leave her audience with all of the tools to dismantle the hell they are experiencing but does highlight the disenfranchised history it has charted. By calling out the economy and the unfairness pervasive in the political landscape, she again seeks to critique the American Dream itself and the "check it still fails to cash." Again considering Royster (2003), while the rhetor must craft a speech that offers to transform this landscape by taking a position of power and authority, Harris leaves her charge to *the people* to dictate the appropriate response. Harris proffers agentive voice to *the people*. Together, reclamation can happen if they strive toward new ways of thinking, not simply because it is in vogue but because it is the only way a future reality can take shape.

Movement 3: "A Daughter of Oakland"

Amid the supporters carrying signs and crafting chants, the C-SPAN camera pans to a few members of Alpha Kappa Alpha Sorority, Inc., the first historically Black sorority for women. Founded at Harris's alma mater Howard University in January of 1908, 111 years before her historic announcement, they form a sizable base of her audience. Yet in 1908, Black women were not even considered full citizens, let alone capable of imagining a seat at the table of Congress, no less within the White House's Oval Office. Considering this background of a historically Black university education and African American social groups, such as the choir of the historically Black Baptist Church in which she and her sister used to sing, Harris has all the makings of belonging to a Black audience. In particular, she is well able to relate to the needs, hopes, and aspirations of Black women. She is also able to sift through the realities of transnationalism, immigrant parents, and a broader African diasporic and Asian identity.

In order to transcend this difficulty of creating a womanist audience, the rhetor must engage in countermemory and counterlanguage and provide a counterperspective to affectively navigate the counterproductive tensions of cognitive dissonance that misogynoir creates and superimposes upon the Black audience. For example, protowomanist social and political activist Maria Stewart came to voice through the realm of a Black audience. She was gifted at speaking to the needs of a traditionally communal space, while also understanding the importance of specifying a Black woman's embodied presence and consciousness within and outside of it.

Gittens (2018) explains that Stewart's rhetorical strategy transitions throughout her collection of speeches and essays. Gittens argues, "She uses casuistry, dissociation, and rearticulation to confirm herself as sacrificially American through consubstantiation, nobly African by history, and divinely feminine by God. These three conscience identities intersect to create an African American female self" (315).

Instead of constituting an audience specifically for Black women, let alone a Black audience, Harris works toward projecting a more intersectional invitation to those in attendance that affectively functions within a more feminist altruist space, if anything, but functions from the merit of her upbringing as a "daughter of Oakland." The re-creation of the womanist audience is one of the most important pieces of putting together a speech that identifies with the complex narrative that is Black womanhood and Black femininity. More than this, the California location of Harris's audience provides a particular vantage point that is atypical for many other parts of the country. As the settling place of Charlotta Bass's *California Eagle* newspaper and much of her activist work, Harris's success and rise comes more than fifty years later. As discussed in chapter 2, the womanist audience is constituted out of the lack of ability to construct itself in the counterpublic relegated to the "Blacks" and the "women." It is not specifically able to identify simply with the people referred to in normative clauses as they were never considered to have access to these constitutional rights in the minds of the forefathers of the nation. However, *the people* that Harris is working to pull together are multifaced, multilingual, and multigenerational, and they leverage multiple vantage points. They are ontologically diverse and this subversive tactic in the way she identifies with multiple people is a particular strategy many Black women do not have the luxury of using, but Harris wisely leverages.

Movement 4: Identifying Self-Love "Faith, Fidelity, and a Fighting Spirit"

One of the most identifiable ways we can begin to understand Harris's speech is through a Black feminist lens that focuses on intersectionality, instead of through womanist rhetorical approaches that strongly emphasize Black women's ways of knowing and engaging in the world around them. While the teleological aims are similar, the entry points are somewhat different. Intersectionality is a concept theorized by law professor Kimberlé Crenshaw emphasizing the multiple dimensions of oppression that coalesce upon people on the margins, in particular Black women. In 1989, Crenshaw's "Demarginalizing the Intersection of Race and Sex: A Black Feminist Critique of Antidiscrimination Doctrine, Feminist Theory and Antiracist Politics" in the University of Chicago Law Forum was the first essay considering this concept. In the essay, she considers the tendency to perpetuate single-axis frameworks and concepts that theoretically erase/e-race and distort Black women's experiences, limiting broader efforts of feminist and antiracist work in several spaces (1989, 139).

This does not mean that Harris's speech does not give glimpses of womanist concepts, precepts, or a perspective that would benefit the Black community. What an intersectional feminist approach does afford is still a holistic balm for communal healing beyond the scope of any particular audience. However, womanism, in and of itself, is focused on the particularities of Black women's experiences based on the phenomenological truths that encroach upon their ontological situation and the specificity of their existential quandaries. Harris demonstrates that she is a candidate focused on identifying with *the people*. These are a people that represent a melting pot of different cultures, different abilities, different hopes, different dreams, and different identities. Ultimately, the goal in highlighting her rhetorical focus is not to suggest an antiwomanist consciousness but to demonstrate that her fight, focus, and frame of reference is guided within *and* outside of a realm of identity that would produce considerably different choices of speech and strategies of persuasion.

She contends, "I stand before you today, clear-eyed about the fight ahead and what has to be done—with faith in God, with fidelity to country, and with the fighting spirit I got from my mother." Although Harris has what she calls a *fighting spirit*, it may not be built on the same radically redemptive self-love and rejection of whiteness that is typical of a Black woman's strivings toward justice. While it is mired in race-based difficulty, there are other dimensions she must and *should* consider as she re-creates a political future. Neither marred nor tokenized, her version of self-love comes to bear from multiple standpoints. Still, I argue she comes to voice peppered by her extensive experience in Black rhetorical spaces. This extension of who she is cannot and should not be denied, though her entry point does not immediately or consistently seek to close the space of her credibility between her white, male opponents. While this is not the only element of difference in her speech, it is a marked contrast seen beside Chisholm and Moseley Braun.

A womanist coming to voice through the tenet of redemptive self-love sees not only the benefit of a future hope but the inherent salvific power of the Black woman's identity simply as a Black woman. She sings Black girls' songs. She chooses their voice to be heard amid the bustle of the reporters, and she listens for the ebb and flow, or the communal spirit, of the audience to call and respond to her prophetic glance toward an eschatological vision. This is not simply for the future, but it can be recrafted, rebranded, reimagined, and reconstituted for the *here and now*. She may get this vision from the teachings of her mother but she shows the community that vision, not simply in her faith and *fighting spirit* but in her fidelity and rhetorical feistiness. This is evidenced in coming to voice, not "because I love my country" but by believing in herself—regardless.

The fullness of the *in spite of* spirt still exists within Harris's speech and her calling back to "fighting Shirley Chisholm" is seen throughout her political campaign announcement. Black women named and unnamed hold together the consciousness she maintains. To a great degree, her audience is *yet* formed and normed by something else, maybe bigger but certainly more broad and less particularized than a womanist proscription. Is it because she was, in fact, the only Black woman with presidential dreams within this study to graduate from a historically Black university? Is it the fact she was *made* into the image of a historically Black sorority on that same campus? Whatever the case, the onset of her speech is not altogether framed in the same Afrocentric rhetorical underpinnings as Chisholm's and Moseley Braun's but it arguably goes toward an available hope of Afrofuturist womanist vision and transformation. An Afrofuturist politic in the womanist rhetorical imagination does not simply conceive a transformative discursive possibility but actually extends a moment of visualization for the audience to see its reality coming to life and being birthed. It mothers this process, not by using merit of identification as its source but by marking the self as the practical, unbought, and unbossed candidate that is able to live within it.

CONCLUSION

Although time has now shown her words and use of space, place, and position may not have gotten her to the office in which she intended, it did enough to deem her a worthy contender and running mate for Joseph R. Biden. When Senator Kamala Devi Harris announced her intention to run for president of the United States, she strategically used the moral and social stature of the King holiday to do so. This strategy in her political arsenal did not match the same capitalist "wokeness" commodified by white supremacist corporations, but it did signify what she wanted to do with her campaign. After the presidency of Donald Trump was mired in the COVID-19 pandemic, perjury, riots, and evidence of Russian election tampering, Harris's vice-presidential rise opens the door for larger study than is available for a text on Black women's presidential announcement speeches. Yet the core of her speech, along with Chisholm's and Moseley Braun's, is that while they may share ontological space, their campaign announcement speeches draw from particularized political wells of experience that create a formula in its own league. Using womanist rhetorical criticism as a means of making this link, over any other frame, demonstrates their similarities much more than it highlights their differences.

Black women standing as candidates for the American presidency creates messaging that is unique. In the instances studied in this text, they offer insight and inspiration that tends to the needs of everyone willing to join their charge for change. Kamala Devi Harris and the very existence of her campaign as a multidimensional rhetor, her function within and outside of the standards espoused and explored within this volume, expand conversations of Black women political communicators. In the same way that the method of merit is calculated by particular measures, and certain methods and messages are valued as virtuous and voted to be meritorious, womanist rhetorical theory outlines certain rules of engagement that benefit all of *the people*, starting with the ways in which they constructively and productively begin with Black women in mind. Without the space or the place for full dismissal of structures that oppress Black women, men, children, and the communities that are wholly and holistically advocating for their survival, while also understanding the bounds of their oppression and marginalization, a true Afrofuturistic womanist or Black feminist vision for "what can be" is impossible. The incompleteness of what still *is* and the foundational steps of what structures must *yet* be destroyed still plague the temporality of a presidential campaign announcement speech, let alone the moment in time of an American political landscape that favors racist, misogynist, sexist, ableist, classist, xenophobic, nationalistic, solipsistic, and transphobic communicative lenses that place Black women's issues and concerns on the back burner.

The possibility to see into the future only begins when we constructively journey toward the past through traditionally affirming communal places, crafting audiences that know the sound of our voices and then coming to voice in the spaces re-created and reimagined with these things in mind. Radical subjectivity or, in this text, the recrafting of a political backdrop does not seem to be enough from the historical precedence of womanist work. Yet to move beyond revisionist fashions of theory, Harris's embodied rhetorical presence drastically shifts every common rule of presidential campaign rhetoric. Just by audaciously standing in the space, she transforms it. While her message quixotically flirts with an Afrofuturist womanist polis, she does not operate within what is immediately a recognizable purely Afrocentric or womanist conscientization. However, the element to reimagine this process and transform the backdrop of Oakland City Hall and the audience before her into a new realm of hope and possibility for thriving is strikingly bold and audacious.

In my original analysis to track a notable womanist style or pattern within the rhetorical persona of Vice-President Harris, her announcement speech simply did not "fit." Aspects of her speech and style change drastically simply because of her location. The audiences of the Black Church and HBCU are so similar and cannot be re-created. However, it may not need to fit the traditional blueprint and rubric. Quite possibly, like in other realms of society, Harris is creating a new shift. Thus, by reconsidering what she is attempting to do and reimagine at the steps of Oakland City Hall, I believe her Afrofuturistic considerations of what her body *is* and *could be* at those specific steps leaves a wide realm of possibility. This is the era of moving beyond surviving and truly leaning into the thriving and reconstructing as noted by Coleman. The bricks are now in her bag. It is her choice. Essentially, Harris ebbs and flows within, without, and quite possibly *beyond* what we have come to know traditional womanist rhetorical style to be. Due to her formidable effort to re-create a diverse audience in front of a space that is typically reserved for the traditional public to stake claim, she boldly stretches the boundary, whether it is helpful or not. It is a boundary heteropatriarchal whiteness has generated but one that her counterparts, Chisholm and Moseley Braun, have actively challenged in their own political service. By an initial detailing of her speech, in and of itself, there is a loose alliance of a Black audience. The would-be womanist or Black feminist participants at the backdrop of her efforts communicates something altogether different. Using Oakland City Hall seemingly dismantles her ability to reconstitute or reconstruct her voice but I would argue that she also sees herself as the individual that stands upon all of the other Black women's shoulders who have gone before her in this journey, regardless of party. By taking a chance, her speech opens a door to another realm of opportunity.

Throughout her speech, Harris determined herself as a credible figure with the means to apply a healing balm for the atrocities and everyday experiences of Black women and the community members they love most. While Harris does well to invite and align herself with intersectional techniques and identification, she also makes purposeful use of what can be considered a dual use of womanist and Black feminist approaches. She indirectly persuades her audience that she is the voice of reason and repositions *the people* as the arbiter of justice. Though this is not a negative action altogether, in a race for president, the rhetor, whether the incumbent or challenger, must demonstrate that he or she is the sole voice to be heard and that can effect and affect strides toward change. Political practicality aside, her backdrop desires a more drastic resolution and reimagination of the future. Her speech is visually situated as an idealistic vision to remove the stigma from a place that has structurally disenfranchised Black and Brown people. The speech itself, both orally and textually, did not necessarily have the momentum to move into the White House but it did find her as second-in-command. Harris, as the rhetor, does not elect herself as the clear leader, visionary, and *fighter* for the people she works to take charge of and break through liminal space. However, *the people*, now for better or worse, have taken notice. Quite possibly, hers is a legacy that leads toward the next steps of transformation with much to remain charted on the steps of many city halls.

Chapter 6

"Daring to be Herself"

Using Black Women's Presidential Campaign Speeches to Create a Theoretical Imperative to Shape the World and a Quasi-Optimistic Future

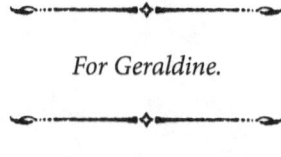

For Geraldine.

CALLING THE ROLL

Alma. Karen. Joyce. Lisa. Corrine. Julia May. Donna. Yvette. Eva. Valdez. Donna. Marcia. Jahana. Sheila. Eddie Bernice. Brenda. Stephanie. Robin. Carolyn. Brenda. Barbara. Ludmya (Mia). Denise. Lucy. Carrie. Juanita. Gwendolynne (Gwen). Eleanor. Ilhan. Stacey. Ayanna. Laura. Terry. Lauren. Maxine. Diane. Bonnie. Frederica. Kamala. At the time of this research, these were the names of the Black women serving in the US Congress. Listing their names here does not simply recognize their political astuteness but brings to the fore the sacredness of their humanity.

Ngade (2011) explains, "Names (especially personal) and naming culture confer identities crucial to maintain power and resilience against the foraying of culturally inherited values in Bakossi" culture (111). That same importance has been adopted across the diaspora and specifically within this text. Calling the roll of the women above not only invokes their presence and power, but because they are political leaders who have, in some way, transcended the rhetorical constraints of American civic life, they should be listed and respected for their stamina, strategic communicative abilities, and the value they represent within a womanist rhetorical framework within political communication studies. More than this, naming them demonstrates how short their tenure in leadership has been in this country. Naming Black women throughout this text, citing them over and against others works through womanist theory and moving away from those within the center, is an embodied methodological move. As such, the analysis effectively centers on dismantling the long-expected need and desire for cultural and communicative credibility to be negotiated away from the marginalized political voices being studied, which traditionally disempower them.

Amid the forty-five articles populated from a preliminary search for "Black women" and "politics" in the Communication & Mass Media Complete during the penning of this study, not one article focused on telling the tales of the presidential aspirations of Shirley Chisholm, Carol Moseley Braun, or Kamala Devi Harris individually or collectively. In spite of their historic firsts, impressive influence, and presidential potential, a simple search produced only five more articles than Black women who have served in Congress since 2000, indirectly or directly, or discussed the broad scope of the field of "politics" in regard to Black women. None of these other women were mentioned. With the exception of first lady Michelle Obama, quite frankly, no other Black woman in politics of high rank was an immediate emphasis. Beyond these names is a field of other women who have spoken from pulpits, podiums, and platforms that have wrestled with the phenomenological truths that impose great difficulty upon Black women's voices and bodies. While women like Maria Stewart challenged the status quo of her day, to suggest that 2020 would provide a starkly different reality for Senator Harris as a presidential contender is, unfortunately, not the case.

From the year 2000, there have been forty Black women who have served in the US Congress. Their names head this chapter. The hope is that the publication process and election cycle will prove that more are to be added. At this time, only one has been elected as a senator, and only one is a Muslim woman and immigrant. The intersections of Black femininity and womanhood pepper these pages in the rhetorical displays of prophetic vision, theoretical practicality, and glimpses of eschatological hope. Black feminist philosopher Angela Davis once said, "Black women have had to develop a larger vision of our society than perhaps any other group. They have had to understand white men, white women, and black men. And they have had to understand themselves. When black women win victories, it is a boost for virtually every segment of society" (1989, 138). Yet, as their conversation suggests, there can be a certain level of danger in their power. Their involvement in buttressing more progressive politics is arguably motivated by their own need and desire to obtain equality; the goal certainly cannot be to save everyone at the expense of their own safety, security, and success. Here again, the social exposition provided by Hurston's character Nanny serves as an incessant reminder that it is not the purpose of Black women to push toward every mark that only celebrates the crosses they alone bear. However, amid the racist, xenophobic, sexist, classist, elitist rhetorical vitriol freely exercised in our society today, we see countless examples of how Black women are losing and not winning.

From #MeToo to #BlackLivesMatter to #TakeEmDown901 in Memphis, Tennessee, Black women have been at the forefront of challenging institutionalized whiteness and systemic patriarchal structures that rape, kill, steal, and destroy. Doing the work of an idealized intersectional feminist agenda, I suggest many of the Black women centering local, state, and national politics would call themselves womanist if the language were more accessible and acceptable. Black women like Tarana Burke, Alicia Garza, Patrisse Cullors, Opal Tometi, and Tami Sawyer have been the progenitors of modern civil rights, while others have been credited by their celebrity or highlighted because of their economic reach.

For the women heading this chapter that have been elected to the US Congress, there are hundreds more that would benefit from not only knowing the sounds of their voices but having the validation of self to understand clearly that they can be rhetorical critics. Whether they become political agents of change with visions of reconstructing presidential futures or in the halls of Congress, their strides to do this as Black women are different than the counterparts surrounding them. The fundamental steps they take toward office do not simply begin with believing they can run for office but are formed by the ways in which their lives are shaped by systems of race, class, gender, and more. A feminist style of speech, by common definitions and displays, does not fully demonstrate what they are contesting within the institutions they are working to enter and, quite often, alter. Contrary to the civil and communicative comforts afforded feminist analytical aims, the goal of a womanist rhetorical criticism follows the range of Black women's experiences. It is not in an effort to reduce them through the typical understanding of essentialism but noting that refusing to point out these isms that are essential to who they are, what they are, and why they are fighting to be heard misses the mark of their full rhetorical lens. Working through the tenets of womanism and operationalizing a womanist methodology also opens the door to understand and hear the song of her possibilities for future research.

For example, Memphis activist turned Shelby County commissioner Tami Sawyer utilizes womanist rhetorical style to move the argument of historically racist monuments toward projecting a campaign for a new vision of Memphis. She was elected shortly after the historic stand she and countless others made in removing Confederate statues in Memphis, Tennessee. As the clear leader, she organized and led a movement that was backed by many challenges. Yet she was not only radically subjective, truthful, and honest but moved well into what she conceived to be a possibility for future generations. Succeeding in this movement, Sawyer garnered her training as a former law school student and Department of Defense employee to tackle the archaic political system and won. Yet examples like this extend beyond the city of Memphis, and womanist rhetorical productions are not only necessary to witness and study on the local level. They are necessary at all levels of governance. This book takes the charge of beginning at the top with Black women who dared to see themselves as president of the United States of America.

A BLACK WOMAN FOR PRESIDENT: AN END TO A POSSIBLE BEGINNING

For Congresswoman Shirley Chisholm, the time was ripe for her to set forth her prophetic vision for a world that on the one hand was beginning to be integrated into many levels of business, military, educational, and institutional work. Following the 1964 Voting Rights Act and the assassination of a prophet of the people, Chisholm worked hard to rise to the occasion as the sole Black or female candidate in the race of 1972. Her speech was one of the first official womanist political speeches in our Western cannon in my consideration. In many ways, the brilliant use of both traditional, womanist, and Afrocentric rhetorical appeals and her investment in a Black audience spoke to her ability to illicit change in her community and put her in a different class of political rhetors. While she did not win the nomination, she blazed a still unmatched path for the Black women who would follow, arguably performing better overall than Moseley Braun or Harris's initial effort.

At the height of the war on terror, Senator Carol Moseley Braun sought to position herself as a practical candidate against an impractical political reality and on what proved to be an impossible stage. She, too, had the experience, firsthand to "right wrongs" and understood the plight of court-ordered school integration in her own city and across the nation. This reality speaks beyond her particular moment in time of giving her announcement speech in a prophetic manner but also lends itself to being a practical solution to moving beyond the positionality of poverty, which is automatically assumed of raced and gendered bodies. Furthermore, her political tenure lends potential for a practical push toward "justice for all" and critically engaging the world around her to have an expanded capacity for greatness, even for herself. This is not simply because we *still* have not seen this prophetic hope of Black women fully elected into power in the highest realms of political leadership come to pass. It is because we *still* have a dire need to believe it is true and that Black women's voices, perspectives, and presence are needed in the highest office in American governance. Using a politics of practicality only made possible through the prophetic imagination of Chisholm, Moseley Braun pushed the womanist political speech in motion with more fervor, in spite of not being drafted for the job.

Then, some two years after former president Barack Obama served as the first commander in chief of African descent, Senator Kamala Harris worked her way into the political limelight for her own strivings toward revisioning and reconstituting space for an intersectional audience to be included and centered in the political trajectory of this country's possibilities for justice, fairness, equality, and hope. Harris, unlike Chisholm and Moseley Braun, did not immediately follow a decidedly traditional womanist vision for the future, though there are elements of her speech that do fit the womanist project. It is not simply the language that is being translated but the way in which the rhetor allows the speech to transform the audience with their voice, embodied and empowered, as the leader that understands, in the most nuanced ways, and how to hear and listen for the needs of the constituents that look most like her. While her speech does not follow my immediate proposed definition of a womanist speech, it does open up the conversation regarding the Afrofuturist political possibility and imaginary through reconstructing, with new bricks, a way forward from systems, structures, spaces, places, and policies that demonize, depress, and dispossess Black women, men, and the communities that advocate their mental, physical, spiritual, and intellectual well-being. Whether or not her vice-presidential legacy will uphold the rhetorical vision she re-created in her announcement speech will be better assessed years after her tenure.

A question that exists underneath the clear inquiries posed for this charge is: Is it *truly* possible for a Black woman to become president? More importantly, can a Black woman dare to be herself in such a public moment and with a womanish disposition? At this point, we do not know. However, based on the speeches we have at our disposal, with the exception of Charlene Mitchell and Lenora Fulani and Cynthia McKinney, we can *yet* hope and cast an imaginary for the vision these women were able to gather for their audiences. In spite of their failure to obtain the nomination, all three women produced considerable attention and proceeded to do what may be, at this time, impossible through a generally conducted election. This did not deter their efforts or their will to look at potential failure as a welcomed challenge.

Other questions left unanswered are, Can Black women in politics utilize a womanist rhetorical framework to get elected? What is at stake when Black women use womanist discursive techniques in their campaign announcement speech construction? Because Black women are always and already placing their bodies in a state of triple jeopardy due to their reality of tripartite oppression, the intersections of their voice, bodies, and intellectual property are often not within their control. Therefore, to utilize a womanist standpoint, one that centers their voice, likeness, and hopes for the future, may very well open up a value of truth and potential. Hence, in spite of their inability to eradicate all rhetorical barriers, their work to deconstruct political spaces that supported white supremacist, racist ideology afforded their voices to be heard, as they dared to be themselves within their own measures.

In the review of the announcement speeches, I contend each woman builds from the words of the generational leader before her. Chisholm ends her speech with a religious perspective in saying, "We are all God's children," possibly paying homage to the speech of Charlotta Bass, who frames African Americans within the Exodus narrative as characteristic of African American religious rhetoric. She captures this by saying, "Let my people go." Moseley Braun and Harris take up the stance of "fighters," albeit in different ways, thinking well of Chisholm's own quest to stand alone as *fighting Shirley Chisholm*. In an unfamiliar space and speaking in unwritten, uncharted territory, their speeches rebuild and reimagine new ways a liberative reality can be forged.

In an interview titled "Memories of *Brown v. Board of Education*—Carol Moseley Braun" with Julian Bond (2014), Moseley Braun spoke about her journey as a civic leader, all infused by her embodied experience of being a Black woman in the United States. Too young to truly understand the full dynamic of *Brown v. Board of Education*, much like Chisholm, Moseley Braun expresses that she did not remember the extent of the historic case and its national reach. However, she states that she was "acutely aware of the efforts of people to build and integrate society" because of the diverse frame of thought and experience in her family and immediate community (Bond 2014). In her presidential announcement speech, she argues that her perspective not only is "practical" but "builds bridges" and "partnerships" with others, as opposed to breaking relationships and trust. What is particularly striking about the language she chooses, in this speech context and others, is her appeal to a wide audience, while also considering her specificity in being cognizant of her historical roots and identity as a Black woman.

Although Moseley Braun's speech, on the outside, seemed practical, as she consistently framed herself as a reliable, steady, moderate choice that could reach many diverse groups, she played on the ideographs and political legacy Chisholm constructed and stood for during her candidacy, campaign, and career. Not only does she discuss her time working for educational reform, but she also speaks of the way in which she has built what Chisholm speaks of as coalitions but Moseley Braun calls "partnerships." This wordplay through her use of alliteration in that particular section is practical and stands out for her listeners, but it also extends an olive branch to those that may be shutting her out politically and/or socially. By following the ideological verbiage of Chisholm, Moseley Braun considers the backdrop of her speech at Howard University along with the audience that sat behind her and before her in "those great halls" but carefully thinks through Chisholm's dedication to the community and her efforts to move outside of it to build relationships and a platform of advocacy outside of it.

Statistics from 2003 and 2004 demonstrate that not only were Black women economically and educationally disadvantaged in comparison to their white counterparts (both male and female), but their narratives were still chained to liminal tropes subjecting them to stagnant rhetorical and political positions. For example, "The three key reasons why media misrepresentation should not be dismissed as simple entertainment are (a) lack of exposure, (b) lack of diversity of representation, and (c) reinforcing notions of difference" (Rousseau 2013b, 460). "These conditions facilitate social rhetoric being used to understand the group, to explain their behaviors, and eventually to justify the regulation, domination, and control of the pop" (460).

In Rousseau's (2013a) summation, historical womanist theory "situates Black women as a unique racialized, and gendered laboring class in the US is developed. Phase one illustrates how Black women have been historically contextualized as instruments of production. Phase two is an expansion of the first phase and shows the sedimentation of Black women's status as instruments of production through processes of racialization and racialized patriarchy. In turn, the third phase of theory development establishes historical womanism as an important theoretical construct and guiding lens that illuminates the contemporary status of Black women" (191).

Black women are always and already seen, viewed, and heard as productive members of society only when their bodies, voices, and messages profit the populations through service, servitude, and smiles. On the surface, Harris's message seems to be mired in the method of merit, but quite possibly that is what she wants the public to perceive. By looking back to the role of Black women political giants that came before her, Harris stands upon their shoulders in an optimism they were not provided. The desire is to have her announcement speech do what is thought to be impossible and improbable: to win. In the same way Shirley Chisholm stood before the people a candidate with charisma and a résumé to succeed, Harris's supporters most likely felt a wind of hope similar to what they had seen in Barack Obama when he was a senator giving the 2004 Democratic National Convention keynote. Young, witty, and a break from the status quo, Harris charged onto an impossible stage just like Chisholm and Moseley Braun.

In spite of her political, positional, and persuasive reality, Harris systematically positions herself in a place that projects her presidential aspirations beyond the temporality of this time but does not disrupt the normative standard through a purely womanist rhetorical vision. Charting an Afrofuturist womanist political imaginary holds the rhetor to a very strict standard that probably has not been possible on the national platform and may be fairly plausible in smaller community strivings. With this in mind, I argue that an Afrofuturist womanist political vision goes forth to see that all organizing, particularly on such a grand scale and with the project of reconstructing such a destructive place as the city hall, (in general) stands for something powerful and looks to be impossible. It also understands that the analytics, assumptions, and ideals of Afrofuturism help us understand our ability for what Harris is trying to do in order to move forward and away from our current reality but also move toward our collective possibilities. Within her campaign announcement speech, not only do we see rhetorical glimpses of these hopes for disruption, but we receive a glance into ways in which we can understand a womanist rhetorical theory as a disruptive rhetorical ethic that elevates embodied discourse as a rational possibility for the political futures we have yet to see, experience, or even theorize. This, through the promise of Sankofa, gets us beyond the metaphysical abstractions of merit within the political organization.

As Wanda Coleman's sonnet at the top of chapter 2 suggests, there is a choice to take bricks to build or destroy. Harris's choice to reimagine her space and broaden her audience was not a decision created out of a vacuum. Her speech pulls from the bag of bricks by willfully framing herself as the new face of governance. The most powerful, *womanish*, and willful thing she does throughout her speech is *willfully* reposition herself at the helm of what true change can be: *the people*. While the symbolism may have been missed by some, she welcomed the ongoing challenge to grapple with the complexities of an Afrofuturist political imaginary. This active exercise of reinterpreting a way of visualizing a space that communicates misery, though abstract, opened the door of possibility. Despite her announcement speech not positioning her at the top of the leaderboard, what she brought to the political table broke another barrier after her predecessors. In many ways, Harris attempts to pull together the prophetic style used by Chisholm and the politics of practicality offered by Moseley Braun. Becoming the first Black woman to hold the office of vice-president, Harris's 2020 presidential dream was not necessarily diminished or denied but created room for a wider net of dreams to be cast. These dreams and visions have shifted our common experience of what the American presidency is and what it *can be* for those daring to be themselves. In fact, while her 2020 race will forever permeate the way we study political communication and the American presidency, her bid in 2024 as the uncontested Democratic nominee swiftly positioned her as the face of a party that desperately desired to do the work of justice for all. However, her 107-day campaign proved incapable of capturing and clutching the majority of the almost 155 million eligible political hearts of reported voters.

A WOMANISH CONCLUSION: TOWARD BUILDING NEW RAINBOWS OF POSSIBILITIES

Six Black women have now run for the American presidency. Charlene Mitchell set up shop at the Frederick Douglass bookstore in Boston; Cynthia McKinney wore a sweat suit to Mercury Café in Denver, Colorado; and Lenora Fulani delivered her speech in a private home in Shaker Heights, Ohio. Yet as she stands behind the backdrop of her chosen space and in front of the audience that calls her into *being* her persona as a Black woman is re-created, reimagined, redefined, and reconstructed by what she chooses to be her central vision and program. While I celebrate and credit the work of nontraditional political runners for the presidency, the choice Chisholm, Moseley Braun, and Harris made to discursively assert themselves by traditional means does multiple things within scholarship and society. In the course of this text, I have not simply highlighted the theoretical touchpoints through my analysis but worked to demonstrate how these three women took normative party politics "by the horns" and permanently transformed the American rhetorical landscape. None of them won the race to the American presidency but all of them seemingly came closer to the goalpost that is persistently moved.

This project has taken seriously the prophetic, practical, and political possibility of a womanist rhetorical theory and vision by exploring not only the location of Black women's ethos as an undercurrent but the spaces in which it is affirmed and how the rhetor can partake in its creation in bettering public life. The aim of this analysis is not only to lead readers who are scholars, activists, and everyday citizens to a better understanding of Black women's challenges in constructing ethos in their rhetorical acts and the ways in which Black women's political speech formation, construction, and performance have crucially different elements to consider than white, male counterparts. When Black women are not only able to move beyond "half notes scattered" in the axiological space of womanist theoretical framing, as within the Black woman's novel, but also move into political futures that bear need of their leadership qualities, we can move into seeing the prophetic vision truly being lived into and experienced. To be "handled warmly" in Ntozake Shange's design is the cornerstone of her choreopoem *for colored girls who have considered suicide / when the rainbow is enuf*, but it is also the foundational epistemic basis of the rhetoric that will save her and those she loves most. At the height of the 2024 election cycle, with much promise and hope to see a Black and South Asian woman ascend to the Oval Office, *the people* thought it was enuf. Unfortunately, for now, we have not come to the end of a rainbow with promises of gold or goals realized.

Reclaiming bodies, just like reclaiming voice and reclaiming time and reclaiming order *in order* to establish ethos as a rhetor, is a deliberate, yet dangerous project that has various checks and balances. These were consistently levied challenges experienced through the struggles for status and personhood of enslaved African men and women and are still culturally normative today. Diversity, equity, and inclusion (DEI) expert Edwina Wong states, "It is crucial when designing gender diversity interventions to understand that women are not a monolith" (2024, 70), and her words are evidenced by the ways in which several institutions and companies have rescinded DEI policies and protections (which unironically) statistically benefit Black women the least in comparison to most of their counterparts on the margins. This not only dislodges the bricks they obtain from their proverbial (and very real) griot bag but disables and dissuades our ability as affective audiences to be formed to hear their visions of a new world to be born. The very dreams they dream are surveilled and even the peace to bereave the vision undone cannot remain unbothered without a request for more work, and new agendas. Indeed, even their rest, an act of redemptive self-love, is shamed and surveilled.

Simone Browne suggests, in her ideas of "racializing surveillance" and more, the very fact that Black bodies are surveilled by the state is further problematized by the ways in which regular citizens, under the gaze of white supremacy, are "deputized" to become watchmen, keepers of virtue in public, and even some private spaces (2015, 21). In short, ethos is inherently tied to how one persuades an audience by having them "believe" they are a (white) man of character. The current discussions found within contemporary rhetorical theory not only make this point plain but also demonstrate that the integrity, robustness, alacrity, and value of white women's voices, Black men's realities, and everyone in between are not *good* enough to be considered in the polis that is rhetorical theory. Although a remedy was not called for, or suggested, we must begin by uplifting an invitation for an intersectional approach and privileging, favoring, choosing but most of all *believing* those women at the various wells, those women on the auction blocks, and those women's voices that shared all kinds of *Good News . . . for their price is above rubies . . . it is indeed, priceless*. Believe Black women. Hear Black women. Elect Black women. But if you choose not to elect them, let them rest. The little girls are watching and waiting.

For all the little girls standing at the beginning of their rainbows and caught in the midst of the rhetorical condition containing Lina's societal critique from *A Mercy* declaring, "We never shape the world, the world shapes us," womanist reads in political communication offer new tools. As a womanist rhetorician, I see the use of characters from Morrison, Walker, Hurston, Shange, Coleman, and other Black women writers as an axiological springboard to chart rhetorical space for freedom to be explored. Using them, along with the words of ordinary but extraordinary women to help frame this exploration of Black women's presidential announcement speeches and their version of a new world for their audience, helps their wisdom live in perpetuity. Although their ways, wisdom, work, and wit come at the cost of being displayed only to often be dismissed, the weight of their vision demonstrates the heaviness of the change only they can make for a more inclusive, holistic world.

While some scholars of rhetoric have begun to make the womanist rhetorical turn, we have not formally formulated nor constructed specific definitions to chart this theory. Definitions give parameters. Parameters allow space for methodology to be exercised. And methods provide qualified and quantified measurements not simply to help Black women be "in control" but, more importantly, for womanist theory to be charted and legitimized in the constructs, constraints, and particular conditions of the communication canon. Therefore, the purpose of this study tests the political rhetoric of Black women who would and could be president. Whether or not they claim themselves to be womanist rhetorical theorists in the public square, Afrofuturist feminists, Black feminists, or somewhere in between is not the overarching teleological end. What is most important is seeing the links between their words, wit, wisdom, and the way that they *keep on keeping on* with the *in spite of* spirt they dare not leave behind in the purses they carry, the pumps they wear in stride, and the podiums, pulpits, or platforms they transform.

In conclusion, this project extends the charge to not simply consider political communication from this womanist lens but situate womanist theory as a metatheory for rhetorical studies. Historically, Black women have had to build from the bones and remnants of heteronormative sources entrenched in patriarchal pontifications that serve them no favors or protections. Yet formed beyond the gaze of whiteness and crafted from the perspective of the mothers, grandmothers, aunties, godmothers, othermothers, Church ladies, and prayer warriors of their communities, churches, and trusted places, womanist rhetorical theory allows Black women to speak truth to power, shape an audience of their own liking, think beyond the limitations of historical caricatures, and extend a mandate that they never be misunderstood but instead come to voice through a radically redemptive, righteous gospel of love. With womanist rhetorical theory shaping the way we theorize visual, oral, and written communication for Black women, the road ahead can be navigated by a map, legend, and helpful notes that help Black women as political leaders or simply as members of the polis to dream, decide, and dare to be *herself* with bricks of her choosing. Still, this era's penultimate question remains: "Can a Black woman be successfully elected as president of the United States?"

For the people or for the status quo?

During the 2024 presidential election, the United States became the closest it has ever been to witnessing a Black woman as president. Certainly, former vice-president Kamala Devi Harris served, if only for moments of protocol and procedure for President Biden, as commander in chief. Such technicalities and the countless unmentioned hurdles Harris undoubtedly had to overcome unfortunately go beyond the bounds of this study. For 107 days, Harris was catapulted to the stage as the uncontested Democratic nominee for president. Yet a myriad of exit polls tell a narrative of the encapsulation of an American public pleasure to not only maintain the status quo but "double down" on its efficacy for another round. Again, although the wide scope of this text cannot venture into the demographic breakdown of voters who did not embrace the idea of actively casting their dreams toward a ballot *for the people*, it cannot be understated that Harris's 2024 run showed similarities to Clinton's 2016 end strength in several ways. Despite not existing within the more populated demographic bloc of voters, the Center for American Women in Politics underscored a commonly understood narrative: Black women, Latinas, and educated white women supported Harris's presidential run (2024). The 92 percent spoke and stood their ground decisively. Such figures should cast light on not what the country is but the hopes of what the country could be.

Harris's 2024 election hopes ended not in failure, but in forcing us to reconcile our faith in what is acceptable in what many would like to consider a meritorious political backdrop. The playing field simply is not equal and indeed can be revised. In large part, with the Democratic party's hope for reelection and the American public desperately demonstrating (in several areas) a need for change, new ideas, and stability amid a war-torn world, Harris positioned herself as a credible leader, with the same overqualified, unblemished résumé Black women laboriously offer from institution to institution. And while presidential announcement speeches cannot actively change the conditions of our world in and of themselves, they can provide a critical glimpse into the ways the women and men who create them can re-create or maintain mantels of leadership within executive policies, politics, position, and promise.

All in all, Chisholm, Moseley Braun, and Harris worked to redefine normative ideas of presidential power and praxis, simply by daring to run in the political race. Their campaign announcement speeches projected countless rallying cries for aligning with the constitutional dilemma of liberty and a better future for all citizens, with a metaphorical hand over every American heart that encompassed justice for all. These three women continued to serve in various positions, despite not receiving the nomination, with Harris serving her fare due with rest outside of the immediate public eye. Within this hope and beyond it, we, as writers, academicians, activists, readers, and citizens, must begin to consider how Black women can function and fare as rhetors in national, state, and local political office. This book ends by calling forth the critical and wisely subversive need to create space for Black women to be seen and heard and celebrated and venerated beyond the racist slurs, misogynist stereotypes, and classist scare tactics so they can become the women they have dared to dream that they can be. Maybe then, outside of the boundaries of our race, gender, class, or other specific stratifications based on the rhetorical constraints thrust against us by heteropatriarchal normative perspectives, "a Black woman for president" will not simply be a hope but a welcome and successful reality.

References

African-American Migration Experience. 2020. "Caribbean Migration." https://www.inmotionaame.org/texts/index.cfm@migration=10&topic=99&type=text.html.
Ahmed, Sara. 2013. "Making Feminist Points." https://feministkilljoys.com/2013/09/11/making-feminist-points/.
Allen, Brenda J. 2002. "Goals for Emancipatory Communication Research on Black Women." In *Centering Ourselves: African American Feminist and Womanist Studies of Discourse*, edited by Marsha Houston and Olga Idriss Davis. Hampton Press.
Alston, Monika R. 2006. *Womanish Ways: The Rhetoric of Black Women Politicians*. PhD diss., Pennsylvania State University. ProQuest (3229003). http://search.proquest.com/pqdtglobal/docview/305246205/abstract/9C1FF8B549E74CF9PQ/1.
Alston, Monika R. 2007. "'Introducing Womanish Ways': An Invitation to Consider Race and Gender." Paper presented at National Communication Association Conference.
Angelou, Maya. (1978) 2013. *And Still I Rise*. Hachette.
Asante, Molefi K. 2007. "Barack Obama and the Dilemma of Power: An Africological Observation." *Journal of Black Studies* 38, no. 1: 105–15.
Asante, Molefi K., and Deborah F. Atwater. 1986. "The Rhetorical Condition as Symbolic Structure in Discourse." *Communication Quarterly* 34, no. 2: 170–77. https://doi.org/10.1080/01463378609369631.
Asante, Molefi K. 1998. *Afrocentric Idea Revised*. Temple University Press. http://www.jstor.org/stable/j.ctt1bw1kjr.
Asante, Molefi K. 2001. *The Egyptian Philosophers: Ancient African Voices from Imhotep to Akhenaten*. Chicago: African American Images.
Atwater, Deborah F. 2009. *African American Women's Rhetoric: The Search for Dignity, Personhood, and Honor*. Lexington Books.
Bailey, Carol A. 2018. *A Guide to Qualitative Field Research*. 3rd ed. Sage.
Berry, Daina Ramey. 2017. *The Price for Their Pound of Flesh: The Value of the Enslaved, from Womb to Grave, in the Building of a Nation*. Beacon Press.
Bitzer, Lloyd F. 1992. "The Rhetorical Situation." *Philosophy and Rhetoric* 25, no. 1: 1–14.
BlackPast. 2007. "(1832) Maria W. Stewart, 'Why Sit Ye Here and Die?'" https://www.blackpast.org/african-american-history/1832-maria-w-stewart-why-sit-ye-here-and-die/.
Bobo, Jacqueline. 1995. *Black Women as Cultural Readers*. Columbia University Press.

Bond, Julian. 2014. "Memories of *Brown v. Board of Education*—Carol Moseley Braun." https://www.youtube.com/watch?v=2Ig50YbDgmo&list=PLKDAfspIjFnJIgKmhotB3DQL5hl4FlcHm&index=1.

Booker, Brakkton. 2015. "How Candidates Announce Can Say a Lot About Their Campaigns." https://www.npr.org/sections/itsallpolitics/2015/04/14/399595210/how-a-candidateannounces-can-say-a-lot-about-their-campaign.

Bowdre, Karen, and Cory Brodnax. 2007. "A Black Camera Interview: Gender Stereotypes in Film and Media." *Black Camera* 22, no. 1: 15–18.

Braun, Carol Moseley. "Moseley Braun on Why Black Women Don't Get Elected." https://www.washingtonpost.com/video/politics/braun-on-why-blackwomen-dont-get-elected/2014/02/26/70b06d32-9ef2-11e3-878c65222df220eb_video.html.

Braun, Carol Moeley. "Carol Moseley Braun Presidential Campaign Announcement." https://www.c-span.org/program/public-affairs-event/presidential-campaign-announcement/119640.

Breines, Wini. 2002. "What's Love Got to Do with It? White Women, Black Women, and Feminism in the Movement Years." *Signs* 27, no. 4: 1095–133.

Brown, M. Christopher II. 2013. "The Declining Significance of Historically Black Colleges and Universities: Relevance, Reputation, and Reality in Obamamerica." *The Journal of Negro Education* 82, no. 1: 3–19. https://doi.org/10.7709/jnegroeducation.82.1.0003.

Browne, Simone. 2015. *Dark Matters: On the Surveillance of Blackness*. Duke University Press.

Burke, Kenneth. 1969. *A Rhetoric of Motives*. University of California Press.

Campbell, Karlyn Kohrs. 1989. *Man Cannot Speak for Her*. Greenwood Press.

Cannon, Katie G. 1998. *Katie's Canon: Womanism and the Soul of the Black Community*. Continuum International.

Cartier, Nina. 2014. "Black Women On-Screen as Future Texts: A New Look at Black Pop Culture Representations." *Cinema Journal* 53, no. 4: 150–57. https://doi.org/10.1353/cj.2014.0050.

Center for American Women in Politics. 2024. "Gender Differences in 2024 Vote Choice Are Similar to Most Recent Presidential Elections." December 28, 2024. https://cawp.rutgers.edu/blog/gender-differences-2024-presidential-vote.

Charléty, Elsa. 2017. "Mules of the World, Unite: The Feminine Black Atlantic of Zora Neale Hurston." Paper presented at Border Crossings: Translation, Migration, & Gender in the Americas, the Transatlantic, & the Transpacific, July 5–8, Bordeaux, France.

Chavez, Leo R. 2008. *The Latino Threat: How America's Obsession with the "Other" Is Damaging Our Country*. Stanford University Press.

Cheng, Yinlong, Anirban Mukhopadhyay, and Patti Williams. 2019. "Smiling Signals Intrinsic Motivation." *Journal of Consumer Research* 46, no. 5: 915–35. https://doi.org/10.1093/jcr/ucz023.

Chisholm, Shirley. (1970) 1989. "Racism and Anti-Feminism." *The Black Scholar* 1, nos. 3/4: 40–45.

Chisholm, Shirley. 1970. *Unbought and Unbossed*. Houghton Mifflin.

Chisholm, Shirley. "Shirley Chisholm: Declares Presidential Bid, January 25, 1972." https://www.youtube.com/watch?v=y3JCX3WxBik.

Chisholm, Shirley. "Declaring Presidential Bid—Jan. 25, 1972." https://awpc.cattcenter.iastate.edu/2017/03/09/declaring-presidential-bid-jan-25-1972/.

Christian, Barbara. 1987. "The Race for Theory." *Feminist Studies* 14, no. 1: 67–79. https://doi.org/10.2307/3177999.

Churchill, Winston. 2024. "We Shall Fight on the Beaches." The International Churchill Society, June 4, 1940. https://winstonchurchill.org/resources/speeches/1940-the-finest-hour/we-shall-fight-on-the-beaches/.

Coleman, Wanda. 1994. *American Sonnets*. Membrane Press.

Coleman, Wanda. 1998. *Bathwater Wine*. Black Sparrow Press.

Collins, Patricia Hill. 1998. *Fighting Words: Black Women and the Search for Justice*. University of Minnesota Press.

Concord Baptist Church of Christ. 2025. "The Concord Baptist Church of Christ History." http://www.concordcares.org/about-us/history.

Coogler, Ryan, dir. 2018. *Black Panther*. Buena Vista Home Entertainment.

Cooper, Brittney C. 2017. *Beyond Respectability: The Intellectual Thought of Race Women*. University of Illinois Press.

Crenshaw, Carrie. 1997. "Resisting Whiteness' Rhetorical Silence." *Western Journal of Communication* 61, no. 3: 253–78. https://doi.org/10.1080/10570319709374577.

Crenshaw, Kimberlé. 1989. "Demarginalizing the Intersection of Race and Sex: A Black Feminist Critique of Antidiscrimination Doctrine, Feminist Theory and Antiracist Politics." *University of Chicago Legal Forum* 1989: Article 8.

C-SPAN. 2019. "Sen. Kamala Harris Presidential Campaign Announcement." January 28, 2019. https://www.youtube.com/watch?v=m4ecapNBaXU.

C-SPAN. 2000. "Kamala Harris Launches Presidential Campaign." https://www.c-span.org/video/?457212-1/california-senator-kamala-harris-launchespresidential-campaign-oakland.

C-SPAN. 2023. "Presidential Campaign Announcement." September 22, 2003. https://www.c-span.org/video/?178291-1/presidential-campaign-announcement.

Curwood, Anastasia C. 2003. *Shirley Chisholm: Champion of Black Feminist Power Politics*. University of North Carolina Press.

Daughton, Suzanne. 1995. "Women's Issues, Women's Places." In *Presidential Campaign Discourse: Strategic Communication Problems*, by Kathleen Kendall. SUNY Press.

Davis, Angela Y. 1989. *Women, Culture, and Politics*. Random House.

Davis, Olga I. 1998. "A Black Woman as Rhetorical Critic: Validating Self and Violating the Space of Otherness." *Women's Studies in Communication* 21, no. 1: 77–90. https://doi.org/10.1080/07491409.1998.10162414.

Davis, Olga I. 1999. "In the Kitchen: Transforming the Academy Through Safe Spaces of Resistance." *Western Journal of Communication* 63, no. 3: 364–81. https://doi.org/10.1080/10570319909374647.

Dery, Mark. 1994. "Flame Wars: The Discourse of Cyberculture." *Utopian Studies* 6, no. 2: 165–68.

Du Bois, W. E. B. 1903. *The Souls of Black Folk: Essays and Sketches*. A. C. McClurg.

Fanon, Frantz. 2008. *Black Skin, White Masks*. Translated by Richard Philcox. Grove Press.

Fensterstock, Alison. 2016. "Essence This Time: A Festival Evolving." NPR, July 12, 2016. https://www.npr.org/sections/therecord/2016/07/12/485707057/essence-this-time-a-festival-evolving.

Fitzpatrick, Ellen. 2016. *The Highest Glass Ceiling: Women's Quest for the American Presidency*. Harvard University Press.

Flores, Lisa A. 2016. "Between Abundance and Marginalization: The Imperative of Racial Rhetorical Criticism." *Review of Communication* 16, no. 1: 4–24. https://doi.org/10.1080/15358593.2016.1183871.

Floyd-Thomas, Stacey M. 2014. "The Faith We Love and the Facts We Abhor: A Response to Lisa Sowle Cahill." *Journal of the Society of Christian Ethics* 34, no. 2: 53–60. https://doi.org/10.1353/sce.2014.0033.

Floyd-Thomas, Stacey M. 2006. *Deeper Shades of Purple: Womanism in Religion and Society*. NYU Press.

Floyd-Thomas, Stacey M., Juan Floyd-Thomas, Carolyn B. Duncan, Stephen G. Ray Jr., and Nancy L. Westfield. 2007. *Black Church Studies: An Introduction*. Abingdon Press.

Foss, Karen A. 2012. "Feminist Communication Theory." In *Encyclopedia of Communication Theory*, edited by Stephen W. Littlejohn and Karen A. Foss, 2nd ed. Sage.

Foss, Sonja K., and Cindy L. Griffin. 1995. "Beyond Persuasion: A Proposal for an Invitational Rhetoric." *Communication Monographs* 62, no. 1: 2–18. https://doi.org/10.1080/03637759509376345.

Fulani, Lenora. 1992. *The Making of a Fringe Candidate, 1992*. Castillo International.

Gaye, Marvin. 1971. *What's Going On?* Tamla.

Gipson, Grace. 2019. "Creating and Imagining Black Futures Through Afrofuturism." In *#identity: Hashtagging Race, Gender, Sexuality, and Nation*, edited by Abigail De Kosnik and Keith P. Feldman. University of Michigan Press. http://www.jstor.org/stable/j.ctvndv9md.9.

Genovese, Michael A. 2001. *The Power of the American Presidency: 1789–2000*. Oxford University Press.

George, Timothy. 2015. "The Sweet Torture of Sunday Morning." https://www.firstthings.com/web-exclusives/2015/04/the-sweet-torture-of-sunday-morning.Gillespie, Andra, and Nadia E. Brown. 2019. "#BlackGirlMagic Demystified: Black Women as Voters, Partisans and Political Actors." *Phylon* 56, no. 2: 37–58. https://doi.org/10.2307/26855823.

Gittens, Rosanna A. 2018. "What If I Am a Woman? Black Feminist Rhetorical Strategies of Intersectional Identification and Resistance in Maria Stewart's Texts." *Southern Communication Journal* 83, no. 5: 310–21. https://doi.org/10.1080/1041794X.2018.1505939.

Gotham, Kevin F. 2007. "(Re)Branding the Big Easy: Tourism Rebuilding in Post-Katrina New Orleans." *Urban Affairs Review* 42, no. 6: 823–50.

Hahn, Daniel. 1970. "The Effect of Television on Presidential Campaigns." *Today's Speech* 18, no. 2: 4–17. https://doi.org/10.1080/01463377009368930.

Hall, Aimee. 1998. "Soldiers Without Swords." https://research-ebsco-com.ezproxy.memphis.edu/linkprocessor/plink?id=edb6ffc6-b6b0-337d-b28d-96d11f856850.

Hamlet, Janice D. 1988. "Understanding African American Oratory: Manifestations of Nommo." In *Afrocentric Visions: Studies in Culture and Communication*, edited by Janice D. Hamlet. Sage.

Hamlet, Janice D. 2000. "Assessing Womanist Thought: The Rhetoric of Susan L. Taylor." *Communication Quarterly* 48, no. 4: 420–36. https://doi.org/10.1080/01463370009385607.

Hanson, Sandra L., and John Zogby. 2010. "The Polls—Trends Attitudes About the American Dream." *Public Opinion Quarterly* 74, no. 3: 570–84. https://doi.org/10.1093/poq/nfq010.

Harris, Kamala. 2019. "Transcript: Kamala Harris Kicks off Presidential Campaign in Oakland." KTVU FOX 2. https://www.ktvu.com/news/transcript-kamala-harris-kicks-off-presidential-campaign-in-oakland.

Harris, Kamala (@KamalaHarris). 2023. "My Message to Black Women and Girls Everywhere: Never Ask for Permission to Lead." Twitter, February 19. https://twitter.com/KamalaHarris/status/1627349063791255553?lang=en.

Harris, Robert A. 2017. *Writing with Clarity and Style: A Guide to Rhetorical Devices for Contemporary Writers*. Routledge.

Harris, Robert A. 2020. *A Handbook of Rhetorical Devices*. https://www.virtualsalt.com/rhetoric.htm.

Harris-Perry, Melissa V. 2011. *Sister Citizen: Shame, Stereotypes, and Black Women in America*. Yale University Press.

Hayes, Diana L. 2010. *Standing in the Shoes My Mother Made: A Womanist Theology*. Fortress Press.

Hill, Rickey. 1994. "The Study of Black Politics: Notes on Rethinking the Paradigm." In *Black Politics and Black Political Behavior: A Linkage Analysis*, edited by Hanes Walton Jr. Praeger.

Hine, Darlene C. 1989. "Rape and the Inner Lives of Black Women in the Middle West." *Signs* 14, no. 4: 912–20.

Hine, Darlene C. 2007. "Ar'n't I a Woman? Female Slaves in the Plantation South—Twenty Years After." *The Journal of African American History* 92, no. 1: 13–21. https://doi.org/10.1086/JAAHv92n1p13.

hooks, bell. 1994. *Teaching to Transgress*. Routledge.

Hopkins, Pauline E. (1900) 1988. *Contending Forces: A Romance Illustrative of Negro Life North and South*. Oxford University Press.

Houston, Marsha D., and Olga Idriss Davis. 2002. *Centering Ourselves: African American Feminist and Womanist Studies of Discourse*. Hampton Press.

Hudson-Weems, Clenora. 1989. "The Tripartite Plight of African-American Women as Reflected in the Novels of Hurston and Walker." *Journal of Black Studies* 20, no. 2: 192–207. https://doi.org/10.1177/002193478902000206.

Hudson-Weems, Clenora. 1997. "Africana Womanism and the Critical Need for Africana Theory and Thought." *The Western Journal of Black Studies* 21, no. 2: 79–84.

Hudson-Weems, Clenora. 2004. *Africana Womanist Literary Theory*. Africa World Press.

Hull, Gloria Akasha, Patricia Bell-Scott, and Barbara Smith. 1982. *All the Women Are White, All the Blacks Are Men, but Some of Us Are Brave*. Feminist Press.

Hurston, Zora Neal. (1965) 2009. *Their Eyes Were Watching God*. HarperCollins.

Jackson, Ronald L., II. 2002a. "Cultural Contracts Theory: Toward an Understanding of Identity Negotiation." *Communication Quarterly* 50, nos. 3/4: 359–67. doi:10.1080/01463370209385672.

Jackson, Ronald L., II. 2002b. "Exploring African American Identity Negotiation in the Academy: Toward a Transformative Vision of African American Communication Scholarship." *Howard Journal of Communications* 13, no. 1: 43–57. doi:10.1080/106461702753555030.

Jacobs, Harriet A. 2009. *Incidents in the Life of a Slave Girl: Written by Herself*. Harvard University Press.
James, Winston. 2002. "Explaining Afro-Caribbean Social Mobility in the United States: Beyond the Sowell Thesis." *Comparative Studies in Society and History* 44, no. 2: 218–62. http://www.jstor.org/stable/3879446.
Johnson, Andre E. "The 'Scold of Black America': Obama, Race, and the African American Audience." *Howard Journal of Communication* 28, no. 2: 174–85. https://doi.org/10.1080/10646175.2017.1290560.
Johnson, Kimberly P. 2015. "If Womanist Rhetoricians Could Speak . . ." *Journal of Contemporary Rhetoric* 5, no. 3: 160–65.
Johnson, Kimberly P. 2017. *The Womanist Preacher: Proclaiming Womanist Rhetoric from the Pulpit*. Lexington Books.
Karenga, Maulana. 2004. *Maat. The Moral Ideal in Ancient Egypt: A Study in Classical African Ethics*. Routledge.
Kelly, Kate. 2020. "Charlotta Spears Bass (1874–1969): Newspaper Owner Who Fought for Civil Rights." America Comes Alive. September 11, 2020. https://americacomesalive.com/charlotta-spears-bass-1874-1969-newspaper-owner-fought-civil-rights/.
Kendall, Kathleen E. 1995. *Presidential Campaign Discourse: Strategic Communication Problems*. SUNY Press.
King, Deborah K. 1988. "Multiple Jeopardy, Multiple Consciousness: The Context of a Black Feminist Ideology." *Signs: Journal of Women in Culture and Society* 14, no. 1: 42–72. https://doi.org/10.1086/494491.
King, Martin Luther, Jr. 1992. *I Have a Dream: Writings and Speeches That Changed the World*. Edited by James M. Washington. HarperSanFrancisco.
Lee, Valerie Gray. 1980. "The Use of Folktalk in Novels by Black Women Writers." *CLA Journal* 23, no. 3: 266–72.
Leff, Michael. 1987. "The Habitation of Rhetoric." In *Argument and Critical Practices: Proceedings of the Fifth SCA/AFA Conference on Argumentation*, edited by Joseph W. Wenzel. National Communication Association.
Lerman, Amy E., and Meredith L. Sadin. 2016. "Stereotyping or Projection? How White and Black Voters Estimate Black Candidates' Ideology." *Political Psychology* 2: 147–63. https://onlinelibrary.wiley.com/doi/abs/10.1111/pops.12235.
Lorber, Judith. 2010. *Gender Inequality: Feminist Theory and Politics*. Oxford University Press.
Lorde, Audre. 2020. *Sister Outsider: Essays and Speeches*. Penguin.
Lorde, Audre. 2022. "The Master's Tools Will Never Dismantle the Master's House." In *This Bridge Called My Back*, edited by Cherríe Moraga and Gloria Anzaldúa. SUNY Press.
McGee, Michael Calvin. 1980. "The Ideograph: A Link Between Rhetoric and Ideology." *Quarterly Journal of Speech* 66, no. 1: 1–16.
Morgan, Marcyliena H. 2002. *Language, Discourse, and Power in African American Culture*. Cambridge University Press.
Morrison, Toni. 2008. *A Mercy*. Knopf.Nelson, Rachel. 2018. "Black Women and the Pay Gap." American Association of University Women. https://www.aauw.org/article/black-women-and-thepay-gap/.

Ngade, Ivo. 2011. "Bakossi Names, Naming Culture and Identity." *Journal of African Cultural Studies* 23, no. 2: 111–20.

Oh, Irene. 2009. "The Performativity of Motherhood: Embodying Theology and Political Agency." *Journal of the Society of Christian Ethics* 29, no. 2: 3–17.

Olopade, Dayo. 2010. "The Root Interview: Carol Moseley Braun." *The Root*. https://www.theroot.com/the-root-interview-carol-moseley-braun-1790878848.

PBS. 2010. "DuSable to Obama: Chicago's Black Metropolis." https://www.pbs.org/show/dusable-obama-chicagos-black-metropolis/.

Pew Research Center for the People and the Press. 2004. "The C-SPAN Audience." March 2. https://www.people-press.org/2004/03/02/the-c-span-audience/.

Phillips, Amber J, Maya Francis, and Chandra Childers. 2018. "Black Women's Political Power and the Savior Syndrome." https://the1a.org/segments/2018-02-07-black-womens-political-power-and-the-savior-syndrome/.

Phillips, Layli. 2006. *The Womanist Reader: The First Quarter Century of Womanist Thought*. Taylor & Francis.

Pittman, Coretta. 2007. "Black Women Writers and the Trouble with Ethos: Harriet Jacobs, Billie Holiday, and Sister Souljah." *Rhetoric Society Quarterly* 37, no. 1: 43–70. https://doi.org/10.1080/02773940600860074.

Porrovecchio, Mark J., and Celeste Michelle Condit, eds. 2016. *Contemporary Rhetorical Theory: A Reader*. 2nd ed. Guilford Press.

Putzi, Jennifer. 2004. "'Raising the Stigma': Black Womanhood and the Marked Body in Pauline Hopkins's 'Contending Forces.'" *College Literature* 31, no. 2: 1–21.

Reid-Brinkley, Shanara Rose. 2012. "Mammies and Matriarchs: Feminine Style and Signifyin(g) in Carol Moseley Braun's 2003–2004 Campaign for the Presidency." In *Standing in the Intersection: Feminist Voices, Feminist Practices in Communication Studies*, edited by Karma R. Chávez and Cindy L. Griffin. SUNY Press.

Rousseau, Nicole. 2013a. "Historical Womanist Theory: Re-Visioning Black Feminist Thought." *Race, Gender & Class* 20, nos. 3/4: 191–204.

Rousseau, Nicole. 2013b. "Social Rhetoric and the Construction of Black Motherhood." *Journal of Black Studies* 44, no. 5: 451–71.

Royster, Jacqueline Jones. 1995. "To Call a Thing by Its True Name: The Rhetoric of Ida B. Wells." In *Reclaiming Rhetorica: Women in the Rhetorical Tradition*, edited by Andrea A. Lunsford. University of Pittsburgh Press.

Royster, Jacqueline Jones. 1996. "When the First Voice You Hear Is Not Your Own." *College Composition and Communication* 47, no. 1: 29–40.

Royster, Jacqueline Jones. 2000. *Traces of a Stream: Literacy and Social Change Among African American Women*. University of Pittsburgh Press.

Royster, Jacqueline Jones. 2003. "Disciplinary Landscaping, or Contemporary Challenges in the History of Rhetoric." *Philosophy and Rhetoric* 36, no. 2: 148–67.

Schroeder, Pat. 2008. "Pat Schroeder Reviews the Clinton Campaign." https://www.npr.org/2008/05/22/90736316/pat-schroeder-reviews-the-clinton-campaign.

Shange, Ntozake. 1997. *For Colored Girls Who Have Considered Suicide When the Rainbow Is Enuf*. Scribner.

Taylor, Toniesha Latrice. 2009. *A Tradition Her Own: Womanist Rhetoric and the Womanist Sermon*. PhD diss., Bowling Green State University. https://scholarworks.bgsu.edu/media_comm_diss/111/.

Temple, Christel. 2010. "The Emergence of Sankofa Practice in the United States: A Modern History." *Journal of Black Studies* 41, no. 1: 127–50.

Thomas, Linda E. 1998. "Womanist Theology, Epistemology, and a New Anthropological Paradigm." *Crosscurrents* 48, no. 4: 488–99.

Trent, Judith S., Robert V. Friedenberg, and Robert E. Denton Jr. 2011. *Political Campaign Communication: Principles and Practices*. 7th ed. Rowman & Littlefield.

Vaidyanathan, Rajini. 2016. "Before Clinton, There Was Chisholm." BBC News, January 26. https://www.bbc.com/news/magazine-35057641.

Walker, Alice. 1983. *In Search of Our Mothers' Gardens: Womanist Prose*. Houghton Mifflin Harcourt.

Walker, Alice. 2003. *The Color Purple*. Houghton Mifflin Harcourt

Walker, Alice. (1979) 2006. "Coming Apart." In *The Womanist Reader*, edited by Layli Phillips. Taylor & Francis.

Walls, Celeste M. 2004. "You Ain't Just Whistling Dixie: How Carol Moseley-Braun Used Rhetorical Status to Change Jesse Helms' Tune." *Western Journal of Communication* 68, no. 3: 343–64. https://doi.org/10.1080/10570310409374805.

Walton, Hanes, Jr. 1994. *Black Politics and Black Political Behavior: A Linkage Analysis*. Praeger.

Wang, Ze, Huifang Mao, Yexin Jessica Li, and Fan Liu. 2017. "Smile Big or Not? Effects of Smile Intensity on Perceptions of Warmth and Competence." *Journal of Consumer Research* 43, no. 5: 787–805. https://doi.org/10.1093/jcr/ucw062.

Warner, Michael. 2002. *Publics and Counterpublics*. Zone Books. https://doi.org/10.2307/j.ctv1qgnqj8.4.

Watkins, Patricia D. 2003. "Rape, Lynching, Law, and 'Contending Forces': Pauline Hopkins—Forerunner of Critical Race Theorists." *CLA Journal* 46, no. 4: 521–42.

Watkins-Dickerson, Dianna, and Andre E. Johnson. 2019. "'Fighting to Be Heard': Shirley Chisholm and the Makings of a Womanist Rhetorical Framework." In *Gender, Race, and Social Identity in American Politics: The Past and Future of Political Access*, edited by Lori L. Montalbano-Phelps. Rowman & Littlefield.

Watkins-Dickerson, Dianna N. 2023. "Womanist Rhetorical Theory." In *Communication Theory: Racially Diverse and Inclusive Perspectives*, edited by Jasmine T. Austin, Mark P. Orbe, and Jeanetta D. Sims. Cognella Academic Publishing.

Weiss, Jacqueline. 2018. "Here's Why Aretha Franklin Always Carried Her Purse on Stage." August 17. https://www.businessinsider.com/aretha-franklin-purse-paid-in-cash-2018-8.

Wells, Ida B. (1892) 2014. *Southern Horrors: Lynch Law in All Its Phases*. Floating Press.

Williams, Delores S. 2013. *Sisters in the Wilderness: The Challenge of Womanist God-Talk*. Orbis Books.

Wong, C. Y. Edwina. 2024. *Between the Cracks: Looking Beyond White Feminism in DEI Interventions for Women*. PhD diss., University of Groningen.

Yaszek, Lisa. 2006. "Afrofuturism, Science Fiction, and the History of the Future." *Socialism and Democracy* 20, no. 3: 41–60. https://doi.org/10.1080/08854300600950236.

Index

African American rhetoric, 61
Afrocentricity, 4, 46; Molefi Asante, 46; *nommo*, 9, 11
Afrofuturism, 111, 116–18, 139
Afrofuturists, 111, 115–18, 124, 128–29, 136, 139, 142
American presidency, 3–4, 8–9, 11, 16, 22–23, 44, 62, 90, 106, 129, 140
Angelou, Maya, 18, 79
Aristotle, 39–40; Aristotelian work and concepts, 23–24, 72, 79, 86, 91

Bass, Charlotta Amanda Spears, 3, 13, 18, 30, 54, 103, 126, 137
beloved community, 4, 51
Black Arts Movement, 9, 43
Black Church, 55, 74, 77–78, 81–82, 130
Black female political leaders, 9; Carol Moseley Braun, 9, 12, 21, 27, 44, 85, 87, 90, 93, 96, 103, 106, 133, 135, 137; Charlene Mitchell, 8, 136, 140; Cynthia McKinney, 8, 136, 140; Lenora Fulani, 8, 136, 140; Shirley Chisholm, 3, 9, 11–12, 14, 22, 26–27, 36, 38, 45, 60–61, 70, 77, 84–86, 104, 128, 133, 135, 139
Black feminism, 28, 47, 111
Black liberation, 4, 9, 32, 58; intellectual naval gazing, 32; James Hal Cone, 32; theology, 4, 9
Bond, Julian, 137
Burke, Kenneth, 32
Burke, Tarana, 134

Churchill, Winston, 72–73
Clinton, Hillary, 77, 95, 109, 112
Coleman, Wanda, 13, 17–18, 124, 139
collectivism, 61, 82
communalism, 15, 38, 42, 56–57, 61, 80, 104
Cooper, Anna Julia, 3, 44
counterlanguage, 44, 70–72, 81, 84, 87, 105, 125
Cullors, Patrisse, 134

Dash, Julie, 117
Davis, Angela, 133
divine symbolism, 57

Fanon, Frantz, 124
Franklin, Aretha, 20

Garza, Alicia, 134
gender, 8, 11, 27, 36, 38–39, 41, 44, 49, 61, 63, 65, 67, 75, 79, 84, 89, 92–93, 105–6, 117, 134, 141, 144
Gerima, Haile, 117
global feminism, 36, 57

Harris, Kamala, 4, 10, 12, 15, 21, 23, 26–27, 44, 85, 109, 111, 136
hegemony, 22–25, 34, 39–40, 46, 47, 50, 67, 101, 117, 119
historical womanism, 138
hooks, bell, 19
Hudson-Weems, Clenora, 10, 49
Hurston, Zora Neale, 41, 107

intersectionality, 29, 36, 111, 120, 126; Kimberlé Crenshaw, 36, 126

Jones Royster, Jacqueline, 122

King, Martin Luther, Jr., 72, 78, 115

labor unions, 66
Lee, Jarena, 3

Maat, 53, 61
Manifest Destiny, 25
metatheory, 17, 29, 42, 142
misogynoir, 6, 27, 29, 35, 67, 81, 105, 116, 125; queerness, 39

Niebuhr, Reinhold, 32

Obama, Barack, 6, 72, 103, 109, 112, 115, 124, 136, 139

phenomenology, 3, 7, 12, 42, 58, 79, 95, 127, 133
Phillips, Layli, 118
political communication, 8–9, 11–12, 16–18, 23, 25, 28, 32, 52, 61, 75, 84, 86, 90–91, 93–94, 111, 133, 140, 142
political persona, 8, 16, 20, 24, 30, 102
prophecy, 42–44, 51, 57–58, 72, 74, 78–81, 86–87, 90, 106, 111–12, 127, 133, 135–36, 140–41; Andre E. Johnson, 79; Arthur Smith, 79; prophetic discourse, 86
protowomanism, 13–14, 30, 54, 57–58, 125

rhetorical criticism, 5, 14, 47, 50–53, 59, 61, 84, 86, 88, 106, 111, 119, 122, 129, 134
rhetorical critics, 7, 19, 35–36, 52, 134
rhetorical devices, 59, 69–75, 84, 91, 97, 99, 119
rhetorical theory, 5, 7, 11–14, 16–17, 27, 29–30, 32–33, 35–36, 38–47, 50, 53, 57, 59, 61, 64, 67, 71, 82, 86–87, 91, 93, 111, 122, 129, 139–43

Sankofa, 8–9, 11, 20, 111, 115, 117–18, 139
Sawyer, Tami, 134
Shange, Ntozake, 141
social justice, 51, 74, 113
Stewart, Maria, 3, 89, 125, 133

Taylor, Toniesha, 4
Tometi, Opal, 134
transformative justice, 19
transnationalism, 29, 123
tripartite oppression, 10, 18, 37, 41, 45, 49, 104–5, 110, 137

Vietnam, 36, 73, 92
violence, 5, 7, 12, 19, 24, 39, 45, 47, 56, 64, 119

Walker, Alice, 5, 33, 42, 47–49, 86
Waters, Maxine, 121
white supremacy, 22, 68, 87, 141; white supremacists, 5–6, 36, 56, 66, 80, 103, 115, 128, 137
womanism, 13, 16, 24, 28–30, 34, 42, 46–51, 57, 95, 118–19, 127, 134, 138
womanist ethicists, 21, 24; Delores Williams, 31; Katie Geneva Cannon, 21; Stacey Floyd-Thomas, 14, 24, 32, 47
womanist framework, 16, 68
womanist methodological mechanics, 21
womanist rhetorical criticism, 14, 47, 50–53, 59, 61, 84, 86, 88, 106, 111, 122, 129, 134
womanist rhetorical theory, 5, 7, 11–14, 16–17, 27, 29–30, 32–33, 35–36, 38–39, 41–47, 50, 53, 57, 59, 64, 67, 71, 86–87, 91, 111, 122, 129, 139–40, 143
womanist rhetoricians, 4, 11, 50, 142

About the Author

Photo courtesy of the author

Dianna N. Watkins-Dickerson is a womanist rhetorician and itinerant elder in the African Methodist Episcopal Church whose scholarship lies at the intersection of rhetoric, race, religion, gender, and politics. She holds a PhD in communication with specializations in rhetoric and media studies from the University of Memphis, where she teaches religion and women's studies.

Dr. Watkins-Dickerson has received recognition and won assorted awards in academic spaces and social influence. From 2020 through 2024, she served in leadership with the African American Communication and Culture Division of the National Communication Association.